A COG IN THE MACHINE

CREATING YOUR OWN STORY!

CASEY T. JAKUBOWSKI, PHD

EduMatch
PUBLISHING

ISBN: 978-1-953852-49-6

CONTENTS

INTRODUCTION

Who knows a teacher? Are you a teacher? Do you realize that what people bring from their lives into the classroom creates the teacher they are and want to be. Teaching is the ONLY profession where everyone has some level of intense experience with the job. They see the performance, but often not the preparation. Nor do people see the work that a teacher engages day in and out, because we see the visual work. Underneath the visible work exists an onion of layers of so many parts that make up a person. I want to help you use this book as a workbook to help you identify your "Passionate Purpose" which Mandy Froehlich writes about in *The Fire Within* (Edumatch, 2018). Why am I doing this? Because I was burnt out. I left the profession. At the five year mark I bailed. Not on my students, but on the other adults, the system, and the level of personal emotional and mental health issues I experienced after I divorced.

I was demoralized, and I quit. I left K-12 to go into "associated career areas" like adjuncting, and academic leadership. I refound a passion, but it was a tough journey. I'd like for you to take your journey with me, and as we go through this journey, I hope you can, at different levels, find what you need. For me, it was reaffirming my identity, and grounding myself in so many different ways in the way I viewed myself, and my work.

The clear path to identifying your identity is creating your narrative journey. For me, I am fortunate to publicly share my journey. For you, it may be private, and it's okay if you need to reflect!

Homework assignment: Throughout this book, I am giving you permission to write, journal, tear out, highlight, whatever you need to do!

But you have to promise me one critical point:

"I promise, I will respect and disclose only what I am comfortable sharing with others. I will not force anyone to share anything that they do not want to."

Now that we have our "challenge by choice oath" on record, your second goal is to:

OPEN A NEW DOCUMENT ON THE COMPUTER
Or
BUY A JOURNAL

Put YOUR NAME on the top of the first page.
Write this:

"This is my story. It is me. I am proud of the journey I am on, and I will forgive myself and support myself, and not #ImpostorSyndrome my good ideas."

Your second step is to engage with me in the exercises that follow to find you. Find your identity as a teacher. We are going to go deep. We are going to examine through my examples your root elements: family and place and history. We do not arrive as blank papers at college. We arrive with background, color and experiences. We arrive with energy. Let's capture that together! Each of us brings into teaching (novice, mid career, changing career, end of career) different points of view. We often do not find our people because of our demoralizing realities. Yet we must find the good, the anchor, and the "right fit" that career coaches tell us is more important than any milestone we may or may not claim credit for.

Our ability to show "grit" is actually a misnomer, for winners really do quit. And understanding when to quit, and take our talents elsewhere is a good mental health strategy. You did not enter a "teaching job." You entered an education profession. A profession is a pathway, a journey. Jobs are way stations along the way. This book will help you find your center, and address the deep core part of you that wants to be a teacher.

STEP 3: WHY AM I READING THIS BOOK?:
Write it down. Was it to find a passion for the profession again? Some examples may include:
*Were you assigned this text in a high school or college class?
* It was a gift....
* PLN/PLC at work.....
What do you hope to gain from the book?

Alright, now let's turn to the nitty gritty: the teaching philosophy statement and that dreaded question, "Tell us why you want to be a teacher?"

*Insert loud primordial shriek here.

"Why do I want to be a teacher" is rooted in identity, and identity emerges from who you are and the journey you have taken. It cannot be for money and summers off. Education is a burnout profession. Critical, but burnout prone. Do you want to help students? Do you want to have a content job? Are you interested in community and civic minded work?

I want you, now, to get up, get a glass of something, turn on silence, or music, and read and interact. Write, highlight, sticky note. YOU GOT THIS!

[1]
OURSELVES AS TEACHERS

Guiding question: When you see yourself as a "teacher" what do you see?

In this chapter, I look at the roots of identity, and how identity plays a part in the development of us. Think about how your journey to the present has evolved?

BACKGROUND OF THE BOOK

Over the past 40+ years, I have traveled the length and breadth of the state for work and for fun. New York is a great state. It has many nooks and crannies that are unique and attractive for families and people looking for a get-away. I have seen a lot of towns and driven a lot of miles. The places of New York State are its heart and soul. The people are the muscle that makes the machine turn and go, driving towards the goal of survival, hope and success. An amazing part of the state is the local quirkiness of each of the little villages, nestled in among the trees. When you drive along the two lane highway, or the four lane thruway, or the twelve lane Long Island Expressway, you get a sense of people moving to their destination. I want to stop, however and enjoy the journey.

My book is here to talk about the known and unknown of my life in education. Some of the themes I share will be familiar to many. Some of the themes will be vaguely familiar. And some will be alien. My unique story is one of growth and change. Never the same, always moving, and evolving. I share this story to understand how I grew, how I became, and more importantly, to help others who have found themselves on the road of life looking around, and wondering "How did I get here? Where do I go now?" A career is a bit bewildering, and yet we as a society in the west are told to plan out our lives when we are in middle school. If I could look back, and tell myself what to expect, I would have wondered who that person was, and what the heck?

For your perspective, and to help you understand, I am a bit of a polymath. Loosely, I like a lot of different subjects, such as history, geography, and politics, but I also like sciences such as geology, biology, invention, and the entrepreneurial spirit. I like to problem solve and help others make the big, hairy problems smaller and more digestible. Therefore, I take a bit of a circuitous route to my destination. Why? Believe it or not, someone's background, and all the pathways help describe their being. This long winding path reveals my thinking.

Psychologists and scholars in general talk about "schemas" or unexamined assumptions (Ragins & Verbos, 2017). How we, as educators, people, and humans get there is our life experiences, our own parents' experiences, and family influences which trace back centuries. I am trying to raise, and tie, how my upbringing brought forth assumptions, behaviors, and patterns from the beginning until the end. I reflect on life, and the pendulum jolts I have experienced in my life. My parents once warned me that youth is slow, and devastatingly short. I now believe my sooth-saying parents!

PLACE-BASED CONTEXT

The pace of everyday life has changed so dramatically in the last one hundred years. Even quicker in the last twenty! With the invention of the internet, the cell phone, and on demand technology, everything is so much quicker, so much faster, so superficial. New York is an old place. The area that the state occupies has gone through some immense changes and always seems to focus on moving faster, quicker, better. Yet there is a slow tug to observe, to wait, to just be. The juxtaposition between the speediness of the urban areas and the gentler pace of the natural regions is so very jarring. In lower Manhattan, you can find yourself wanting to go super-fast, but caught up in a line or traffic jam, while in Hamilton County, in the heart of the Adirondacks, you may want to go slow, but find the speed limit is 55 miles an hour on the open road.

One of the big ideas most people have about upstate New York is snow. Yet there is so much more. New York has been blessed with wondrous lakes that are calm and clear and refreshing. And the lakes are sitting right there for people to see and experience. Within and around those lakes you can see a multitude of wildlife, including swans, geese, deer, beaver, and trout. But you can also see butterflies and birds like cardinals and loons. The weather in the state allows you to feel the cool breeze coming off of our two great lakes, Erie and Ontario, our finger lakes, and Lake Champlain to the north. What is even better is the ocean breeze that brushes against you as you await the surf along the Atlantic Ocean, your feet touching the cool wet sand of the dunes.

New York has a diverse range of regions. To most outsiders, New York is dominated by two things: the city and....the city. While it is so true that the state does contain the largest urban area of the North American/United States, almost 85% of the rest of the state is not New York City (Thomas, 2012). The regions north of the city are dotted with ponds and interwoven with streams. The areas contain natural reserves that are amazingly large, such as the Adirondack and Catskill State Parks. There is also an architectural and metropolitan grace to the regions north of the City. In my hometown area of Buffalo, there is a cosmopolitan feeling for an area that has Eastern European food purveyors next to Thai restaurants. You can take in the architecture of Frank Lloyd Wright while sipping sake on Delaware Ave, named for a Native American nation. Or you can enjoy Pad Thai while gazing on the Niagara Escarpment after a day of hiking the trails of Goat Island and Three Sisters Island by Niagara Falls. What is amazing is the collection of the people who call New York State home, and fight so passionately for their communities in the wake of economic and social decline that has blighted a once proud state who goes by the moniker "The Empire State."

New York has called itself the home to the first Hamburger (Hamburg), Trico Wiper Blades (Buffalo), cancer treatment centers (Roswell Park), and of course the Buffalo Bills (hey, I'm from Buffalo! I know about the Jets and Giants....who won Super Bowls...). It is the home to a number of great Americans, including presidents (Chester Arthur, Franklin and Theodore Roosevelt, Grover Cleveland). We have some of the top ranked institutions of higher education in the state, including West Point, the Merchant Marine Academy, Columbia, University at Buffalo, Syracuse University, Rensselaer Polytech, New York University, University of Rochester, and smaller liberal arts colleges like Hamilton, Colgate, Niagara, and Canisius. I have personally attended SUNY Fredonia, SUNY Binghamton, SUNY Buffalo and SUNY Albany. I have taught or worked at Niagara University, Buffalo State College, Niagara Community College, Syracuse University, Morrisville State College, and Rensselaer Polytechnic Institute. The state is so diverse academically, with small two year community colleges to large doctoral granting research universities. The state has a large range of local schools, with over 600 school districts serving the smallest number of students (Raquette Lake UFSD) to the largest (New York City Department of Education).

Historically, the state has been the site of epic battles from the colonial times to the present, as protesters have called out the "1%" of the elite. The French and Indian War was fought in our North County, with Lake George and Fort Ticonderoga serving as flash points. The Revolutionary War saw the pivotal battles of Ft. Oswego, Saratoga, and New York. The Sullivan campaign along our Southern Tier destroyed the strength and unity of the Iroquois Confederacy. In the War of 1812, Western New York and Lake Ontario were focal points, as the British and their Allies fought against the Americans. After the War, the border with Canada became the longest demilitarized zone in the world. Many Canadians ski at Kissing bridge and Holiday Valley in Ellicottville, NY. Interstate 87 makes travel between Montreal and New York City easy, convenient, and allows travelers to see the Adirondacks up close.

In the battles leading up to the Civil War and during the Civil War itself, New York provided significantly to the manpower of the Union Army, and held Confederates in Elmira at one of the largest and worst POW camps of the war. Buffalo and Niagara contain a number of Underground Railroad stops, and Watervliet NY (called west Troy at the time) was the site of a famous rescue of an African American fleeing the Fugitive Slave Acts. The Burden Iron Works of Troy provided many of the cannons used during the war. In Stillwater's cemetery, just south of Saratoga, lies Col. Ellsworth, the first Union officer casualty of the war. Across New York, in small rural cemeteries and in large urban ones, rests in eternal peace the dead of the war, lost during battle and after, to wounds, disease, and old age. Our villages contain monuments to the local boys who went to war, came back as men, and to some who never came back and are missed by family, friends, or just citizens who walk by and ask who the memorial stands to remember.

One of our own led the Americans into the Spanish American war, as Teddy Roosevelt gained fame as "Old Rough Rider." These actions became the basis for a Congressional Medal of Honor, or not, depending on what Congress says at this moment. He later became president, as William McKinley was killed in Buffalo at the Pan American Exposition. Roosevelt was vacationing in the Adirondacks, a place made popular for its rustic and scenic beauty.

During the Gilded Age, many of the wealthy of the nation built large mansions in New York City, the Hudson Valley, and in the Catskills and Adirondacks, as the trains took families to the fresh mountain air, and away from the City. Lake George morphed from a place where battles were fought to a tourist destination. The Catskills saw the development of large summer camps for the wealthy of New York to play in lakes and among the trees. The 1980s cult classic, "Dirty Dancing" immortalized the summer camps in this generationally remembered, and award-winning film.

All the while, the state has played home to so many immigrants arriving on the shores of this nation. Their conditions were horrid, and jobs difficult. New York City, Buffalo, Syracuse, Rochester, Utica, Schenectady, Poughkeepsie, and Newburgh contained the burgeoning industry that allowed waves of Irish, German, Jewish, and Polish immigrants to enter the county and find work. The Statue of Liberty and Ellis Island became the first sights for many immigrants to the New World. Neil Diamond's *The Jazz Singer* gave generations the song played at the Fourth of July that stirs the soul, and causes a tear to form:

Far
We've been traveling far
Without a home
But not without a star
Free
Only want to be free
We huddle close

Hang on to a dream
On the boats and on the planes
They're coming to America
Never looking back again
They're coming to America
Home, don't it seem so far away
Oh, we're traveling light today
In the eye of the storm
In the eye of the storm
Home, to a new and a shiny place
Make our bed, and we'll say our grace
Freedom's light burning warm
Freedom's light burning warm
Everywhere around the world
They're coming to America
Every time that flag's unfurled
They're coming to America
Got a dream to take them there
They're coming to America
Got a dream they've come to share
They're coming to America
They're coming to America
They're coming to America
They're coming...

As the First World War emerged, New York played a significant role in the war effort. Not only did the men and women of the state volunteer, but the shipping infrastructure built up the liberty boats to send supplies and men "over there" to fight the Kaiser's army. After the war, as the empires of Eastern Europe crumbled, and the Communist Revolution destroyed the Russian Empire, more eastern Europeans tried to leave, but found that their escape route was clogged. Some trickled in, but not many.

As the 1920s developed, and saw the rise of the golden age of screen and radio, New York City became the home of some of the stars of the nation, and the glamour and glitz of New York City had people hoping to make it on the "Great White Way" of Broadway. The Stock Market boomed, and companies sought to locate in the Greater New York area. Companies like Pierce Arrow and General Electric built large plants in New York State to keep up with growing consumer demand. Then, in 1929, in late October, Black Thursday, Monday and Tuesday wiped out almost 40% of the market's level. When New York City sneezed, the nation caught pneumonia. As the nation tried to cope, the state led the way, and FDR was elected president. Some of his social policies from his time as governor were scaled up across the nation. Many of the smallest schools in New York benefitted from the Works Progress Administration's efforts to construct schools in rural areas in the 1930s. The CCC planted thousands of acres of trees across New York. Robert Moses became a baron of public works, constructing multiple parks, parkways, and paving the way for construction of power plants across New York from Ogdensburg to Fire Island.

Then, as World War II began, New York again led the way. Western New York and Long Island led the way in manufacturing aircraft for the war efforts. Grumman and Republic led the way manufacturing aircraft for the Army Air Corps and the Navy. Remington, in Ilion, NY, provided weapons for the military, in continuation of its almost two centuries of service. After the war, New York became a safe haven for Jewish war refugees, as Fort Oswego became a displaced persons camp, and New York City welcomed fleeing civilians from war torn Europe and Communism. The Carrier Company in Syracuse, NY provided air conditioning services aboard US Naval vessels and manufacturing plants needed for the war effort. In Rochester, Kodak provided the US military with hand grenades and a wide variety of products that assisted in the war effort. Fort Niagara again saw military action, as a POW camp for Germans and Austrians. Long Island's civilians served as sub lookouts, in order to protect the harbor into New York City.

After the war, New York saw the first moves to the suburbs, as Levittown Long Island became the first planned community designed and manufactured to accommodate the growing baby boomer generation. The State University of New York was created, bringing together the State Normal Schools (teacher Colleges) and University at Buffalo, to create an integrated 64 campus organization that is one of the largest in the nation. For many, the state was perfect to use as a launching ground for the Civil Rights Movement, as New York became home to many African Americans who fled the south during the "Great Migration." Jackie Robinson became the first African American player for the Brooklyn Dodgers. In 1969, Hector Lopez became the first black manager in baseball, leading the minor league Buffalo Bisons. New York has as part of its legacy a number of reformers. Frederick Douglass of Rochester, Susan B Anthony, and Harriet Tubman all called New York home. In Seneca Falls, in the 1840s, the Declaration of Rights and Sentiments sent out notice that women deserve equal treatment as men in all matters . Constance Motley, a New York City native, became the first female federal Judge, while Sonia Sotomayor became the first Latino judge on the US Supreme Court. New York City's cosmopolitan nature has led to a large number of gays and lesbians seeking a city that allows free expression of their rights as people. New York became a pioneer in recognizing same sex rights, including the right to marry. Albert Shanker and others led teachers in gaining rights to representation as part of professional associations. The creation of the American Federation of Teachers was born in New York.

As the nation worked through the 70s and the 80s, New York became one of the rust belt regions of the nation. Buffalo, Rochester, Syracuse, Utica, Schenectady, Troy, Binghamton, Elmira, and the

North County experienced population decline and industry fleeing as international corporate mergers saw manufacturing jobs leave for the south and Mexico. New York City went bankrupt, and needed emergency financing in order to function. Displaced workers fled the upstate region for the south and west, and the once wealthy places, such as Buffalo, with the 7th highest concentration of millionaires in the early 1900s, saw its poverty increase. The schools became segregated, as more and more whites fled to the suburbans. In other cities, the school systems in the urban areas fell from excellence into problems. Urban renewal, promoted by the federal government, saw entire neighborhoods destroyed as highways cut apart downtown. In Albany, the Empire State plaza was constructed, with the signature Corning Tower, the tallest building between Montreal and New York City dominating the skyline. In the North Country, and along the Pennsylvania border, the smaller villages became smaller, as older residents died, and younger ones went to larger, more urban areas in search of work. Norwich Aspirin, in Chenango County New York, was sold to a much larger firm and many of the jobs were moved out of the area. Bendix company, in Sidney, Delaware County New York,became part of a series of mergers and sales which resulted in a significant decline in the number of jobs and residents in the area.

In 1988, the Buffalo Niagara Region became enamored with the Buffalo Bills winning ways, as the team started an unprecedented four straight Super Bowl appearances. On Long Island, the New York Islanders were dominating the hockey world with five straight Stanley Cup Finals appearances (and four wins) in the early 1980s. In baseball, the New York Mets won the world series (1986), while the Yankees were in a decade of slumping. The Yankees are the dominant baseball franchise, with 27 wins in the World Series. The New York Giants won in 1987 (and 1991, but I won't talk about that one). Syracuse University dominates collegiate sports in the state, with its lacrosse, football, and basketball program nationally prominent. Recently, the smaller New York schools have seen success in lacrosse and basketball. The New

York Football Giants have won two more Super Bowls, and the Buffalo Sabres hockey team appeared in the Stanley Cup. The New York Rangers gained prominence, as one of the Original 6 hockey franchises, and now have three Stanley Cup Championships.

In the 1990s, the state was faced with one of its most recent challenges, as the Base Realignment Committee proposed closing a significant number of New York State's military institutions. The Cold War was especially good for New York, with a number of military establishments constructed, or old ones repurposed. Major base closures hit New York hard. In Plattsburgh, the Plattsburgh Air base was closed. This created a huge gap in North Country employment. In Utica/Rome, Griffiss Air base lost its active military status. In the Finger Lakes area, Seneca Army depot was closed. Four bases in the Greater New York area were closed, including the historic Brooklyn Naval Yard. While these closures caused pain in the economy and in the social community, some good has emerged. Seneca Army Depot should become a natural preserve and small business incubator park. It is home to the largest herd of white deer in the Northeast. Its location, between Cayuga and Seneca Lake, gives it a number of natural advantages that could allow it to grow. More about it later. In Rome and Plattsburgh, the two former air bases have become industrial parks, where small incubators for industry and small business are trying to attract startups and unique retail and manufacturing firms. New York is home to a number of first response units, and has a proud National Guard heritage.

On September 11, 2001, New York state was victimized by the worst terrorist attacks in the nation's history. The World Trade Center was destroyed, and thousands of New Yorkers and innocent plane passengers became victims of sheer madness. The state reeled, as commuters from Long Island, Westchester, Orange, Rockland, and other counties were killed. The State University System and other colleges across New York lost alumni, as many killed had attended school in the state. Firefighters, police officers, and other first responders died in the events of that day. Across New York, like the nation, mourning still continues to this day.

In recent years, the state has seen growth and development, as the intellectual capital of the SUNY schools have seen the birth of Nanotechnology in the state. The capital area of New York has been rebranded as Tech valley, and Saratoga, long known for mineral water health spas and horse racing has become a focal point for Nanotech manufacturing. In Rochester, the Photonics industry is using the knowledge of Xerox and Kodak to harvest the intellectual base to grow a new field. Buffalo is seeing a rebirth, as the Buffalo-Medical campus is taking older industrial areas and growing them into research facilities. The Central, southern Tier and North County are working on investing in solar and wind energy, as old fossil fuel energy plants are retired. The state has been wracked with divisions between the resource extraction industry and the preservation lobby, as more acreage has been added to the Adirondack park zone, and taken out of potential use by commercial businesses. In the smallest communities, decreased employment, falling populations, and rising poverty have resulted in struggles for survival. How do villages attract and retain young families when the economic opportunities are poor?

The state has seen controversy, as medical marijuana and hydrofracking have divided the state. Political scandals have rocked the capital, but then again, New York is the home of Tammany Hall and the Muckrakers. In presidential tradition, New York became the home of the Clintons, as Hillary Clinton was elected to state senator, then appointed to Secretary of State by President Obama. She has been a declared candidate in the 2008 and now the 2016 election cycle, joining Geraldine Ferraro as history makers on the national ticket. With her loss to fellow New Yorker Donald Trump, we again see a division between what upstate New Yorkers and down state city dwellers see as relevant and important. New York also dealt with controversy surrounding the legalization of gay marriages. Many socially progressive areas within New York wanted to honor their friends, family and neighbors by legally allowing marriages. New York started with civil unions, and then, under Governor Cuomo, pushed through legislation to finally legalize same-sex marriage. This debate rocked the state, and once again divided the conservative upstate areas with the more liberal downstate regions.

As educators, connecting place and curriculum is crucial. We need to ensure that our students understand *where* they fit within the picture of their local school, the region, the state, the nation, and the world. I give you a broad outline of the state for one purpose: New York insists on education. New York is home to, and is critically influenced by almost 700 local school districts, each with their own stories. And these stories are unique from the City that never sleeps (thank you Sinatra for calling New York City this motto) to the tiny Raquette Lake Union Free district in the Adirondacks which services two children by sending them to a neighboring school.

The short, short introduction to the history of my home state will hopefully lay the groundwork for the next series of stories. These stories are organized around my time in different locations across the state. There are places I have lived, visited for fun, or interviewed in. I have lived for over 35 years in one state: New York. I have lived in areas near great cities, worked in and around large cities, but have lived and worked in small communities. When we know where we come from, we become better teachers! We ground ourselves and our place in the world, then the classroom becomes more comfortable. Like a well-fitted hat on a winter's day, it warms us, and we can refill our bucket, replenish our spoons, and get up and become gritty to help our students in their efforts. I recommend strongly that YOU dear teacher prepare yourself for a journey, and remember, this is a joint journey. My leading you virtually via this book, and you remembering the path, or forging your own path, or planning a path.

REFLECTIONS:

- What are some facts about your state (current or former) that you believe influence your view about yourself?
- How has your state or the place of your upbringing influenced who you are as a teacher?
- What moment do you find pivotal from your state or region's history that influences your choices today?
- What song or movie, book, or work of art moves you emotionally? How do you share this emotion with friends, family, or students?

[2]
GROWING UP

This chapter focuses us on family, and how family identity plays a huge role in who we are and what we take with us as we grow into our present self. Make sure that as you are looking at the world, you think about not the biological definition of family, but on your lived reality.

Guiding question: How has your "family background" influenced YOUR identity as a teacher?

BACKGROUND

A strong influence on how I grew and developed, and on many others, is my family. I am proud of my working class, second generation immigrant roots. I also want to share that these roots birthed my love of history, politics, and sociology. My genealogical story also describes how I identify, and how I identify is inexplicably linked with future assumptions, professional practice, and how many others with the same experience became educators. Do not forget, teaching is as

David Labraree describes (2004) in *The Trouble with Ed Schools* (Chicago: U Chicago Press) one profession which allowed working class children to move into middle class stability. Teaching also allows middle class children to maintain middle class status... or at least until the last ten years or so.

Born in Buffalo, NY at Women's and Children's Hospital, I joined a family that had combined just one year earlier, when my parents married at St. Gabriel's Roman Catholic Church in Elma, NY. Dad's family was a Polish group that had settled in Western New York in the late 1800s, as his Great Grandfather Lawrence came to the area from Poznan, Poland. There, Lawrence met his wife Maryanna and had two sons. I am descended from the youngest of the two, Andrew, who was born in Buffalo. The family then relocated to suburban Cheektowaga, into an area dominated by Poles, and attended St. Josaphat's Roman Catholic Church. The census indicated Lawrence and Andrew were laborers. Andrew then met Elizabeth Pietrzak, and married. They had a large family, including my Grandfather Alfred. The family then moved further out to suburban Lancaster, where they farmed a large area while Andrew and Alfred worked on the railroad. Alfred then met Genevieve Chowaniec, and they married and moved into a house in Elma, NY on property owned by Genevieve's father Stanley Chowaniec and mother Mary Czapla, both recent immigrants from Poland. My grandfather Alfred, his brother Andrew Jr., my great uncles Stanley Chowaniec, Frank Chowaniec, and Norbert Chowaniec all served during World War II. Aunt Terry Chowaniec became the executive assistant to Mr. Oshei, one of the owners of Trico. Aunt Charlotte Chowaniec was an executive assistant at Buffalo Wire Works. Aunt Charlotte served as my godmother, and was there for so much of our lives. My Great Aunt Mary Jakubowski was a trusted member of the household staff for some of Buffalo's elite on Delaware Ave. While working at blue and pink collar work, the Jakubowski-Chowaniec family saw the growth of Buffalo's Polonia, especially the Broadway Market, and became founders of St. Gabriel's parish in suburban Buffalo in 1925. My great grandfather Andrew saw firsthand the railroad workers' strikes in the Cheektowaga yard, while the Stickley Furniture Corporation employed his uncles.

Mom's family has a bit deeper roots in America. Her father's side, the Maulers, moved around, with stops in Indiana, Pennsylvania, and other areas that allowed them to see the rise of industrialization. Many of my ancestors lived in Pittsburgh, PA, in steel and in the fire service. My mother, through her great grandmother (Davis), is the descendant of a Civil War veteran, who saw action at some of the worst campaigns including Spotsylvania. This quite large family tree gave rise to a daughter who then married a fellow Pennsylvanian, who later moved to Buffalo as the steel industry grew, especially as Bethlehem and Republic Steel dominated the Lackawanna skyline. Many of the family lived in South Buffalo, and were part of the industrialization that saw the south Buffalo Irish and Germans formed an ethnic identity that is still celebrated in the annual St. Patrick's day Old First Ward Parade and the rise in the Oktoberfests in Buffalo.

My grandfather Mauler was a veteran of World War II. He also served as a member of the US Post Office. My grandmother Catherine worked at a number of jobs, but her proudest was being a grandmother. She had eight grandchildren in all. She had a rough life growing up, the product of a marriage that ended when her mother died. She had an unhappy childhood, and had always wanted to become a teacher. I never knew this until much after she had died, but now I know where I got the teaching bug from: my Grandmother Catherine.

My parents decided to move us to Orchard Park, NY where we lived. The Orchard Park area is named the Quakers due to the influence of the Quaker meeting house in the area. Orchard Park became very suburban in the last decade, but it is still home to horse farms and agricultural roadside stands. It was just suburban enough to have wide open fields where the lake effect snow off of Lake Erie would come howling into the area. When my brother came along in 1980, and we adopted a dog into the family, I thought all was well. Western New York has a strong tradition of loving dogs as family pets, and my father was working on the railroad as a fireman. He was part of the Conrail company, and had spent time working in the Buffalo Central terminal. He frequently worked on the rail line that went from Buffalo to Syracuse. His work took him on the road a lot. It also allowed us to travel to Disney World and experience Sesame Place.

I can remember my grandmother and my two great aunts on dad's side going with us to Disney World in Florida, as we celebrated my brother's birthday in Disney World. My grandmother would take us to Lancaster's Cuomo Lake Park. We would join my great aunts at church fetes and bazaars, tasting the foods of the carnival and the Polish cuisine of the churches. St Augustine's parish in Elma continues to sponsor a Clam Chowder that is divine. I have no idea the recipe, but it is great for a warm August day. The broth is rich and contains corn, beans, and carrots. Time with my family was spent visiting my grandparents a lot on their farm in Elma. My great grandfather Stanley had divided his farm up into plots for each of his children and gave them a start in life. My family was never far away, as we had on Blossom Road, my grandparents' house, my father's brother, his wife and two kids, my great aunts who shared a duplex, some family land, and my great uncle Frank and his wife. The whole area was a playground for younger children who could get into a lot of trouble. As a family we often spent Christmas Eve at my grandparents, celebrating the Wigilia, with foods traditional to Poland. There was always pierogi, barley, rice, peas, carrots, onions and mushrooms, cabbage, stewed fruits and Optak, the Christmas wafer, broken apart and passed around to members at the table in celebration of the health, happiness, and luck each was deserved. We had a crowded kitchen, with my grandparents present, Babcia (Polish for grandmother) in the kitchen cooking, and Dziedic (Polish for grandfather) in the living room talking with my uncles. There was always a real Christmas tree, with old ornaments on them. Traditional polish Koledy records would be playing. There was always a debate or a discussion, about church, the homily of the priest, or the politics of the day. After dinner, we were allowed to open gifts from my grandparents in the living room, and then we would head back to Orchard Park, driving along Transit Road and Southwestern.

Southwestern Boulevard is the sight of the infamous Indy Dog rescue that went wrong. I was a little boy and my brother was a baby under one years old. My dad was out on the road for Conrail, and our dog Indy escaped. Well she ran away on a cold day and my mother was panicking. We went out to rescue her in an old car that didn't get a lot of traction, especially when the snow fell. As we were out driving around the area looking for her, my mom spotted her and pulled over to call her home. As she exited the car and called for the dog, Indy took off with the boy dog she was hanging out with. Mom got back into the car and tried to pull away. Too bad the car was slipping into the ditch. After another driver tried to help us out and got stuck as well, a jeep pulled up and managed to get us out of the stuck situation. That was one of my earliest memories of Western New York, neighbors that will help you, even if they don't know you. I also learned that dogs that run away come back and have puppies! Needless to say, my family had a lot of dogs, so we wound up giving many of the puppies away, except for Indy and her one boy puppy Scottie Dog.

When dad returned from the road trip, he made sure my great aunts and grandparents would check in on us, because he was very fearful that another railroad trip would be a disaster for the family in the drifting snow of Southwestern and Webster Road in Orchard Park. My father's two brothers lived in Elma, on the old family farm. My Uncle Tom, the youngest, went to work for the State as a member of the DOT as an engineer. He moved across the state to Albany, foreshadowing our family moves later. His other brother John and his wife Pat and two children lived in the old Chowaniec family house on the old farm. They would visit sometimes as well, but we went over to the family houses in Elma with huge land and plenty of space to run around. We also had another angel who would guard us, my Godfather Steve Kovac, a South Buffalo outdoorsman who was one of my dad's best friends from college.

Uncle Steve, as we call him, grew up in a Czech neighborhood in Buffalo. He came from a small family. His dad, Mr. Kovac, made amazing Christmas cookies every year. To ensure they were just right, he would turn down the temperatures in his kitchen to near freezing and bath his hands in ice water. The cookies were the best. Steve's mom was an amazing woman, who was strong and would have toys for us to play with. Come to find out, they were toys for her granddaughters by Steve's sister and her husband. Toys, nonetheless, and cookies that were amazing.

Having grown up in a warm family, my godfather Steve loved to hang out with dad after class where they enjoyed the cheap meal of the day: one beer and French Fries. Dad and Uncle Steve, along with another friend Tom Hijduk, were buddies. They would go camping and travel around the northeast. I can remember when I was much younger, Steve, Dad and I went camping at Allegany State Park. This was my first time in a tent, and eating over a campfire. I loved it! That week we went canoeing and I felt the rush of paddling towards the Kinzua Dam. We were miles off from the falls of the dam, but to a small kid, it was an adventure.

Every Christmas morning, and Easter, Uncle Steve would come and visit us in Orchard Park and give us gifts. He spoiled us too much. But my favorite part was breakfast. He and mom and dad would cook a huge breakfast that we would enjoy together. The best part was the Christmas cookies that we were allowed, all because Uncle Steve was over and visiting. One of my most prized possessions is the picture of me as I sat with a huge stuffed teddy bear he gave me. It felt like I was sitting on a throne whenever I sat on that bear. For a bachelor gentleman who liked to camp and travel, he was amazingly devoted to my brother, me, my sister (who comes along later) and his nieces, Jennifer and Tina. Uncle Steve provided a huge help to our family and he is deserving of his name. St. Stephen is a patron saint of Christianity, and a martyr for the church. St. Stephen gave alms and food to the poor and provided charitable relief. My godfather, Stephen Kovac died of pancreatic cancer in his family's home in the summer of 2005. We were there the day he had to go to the doctors to hear the treatments weren't working. The doctors do not know why he died of cancer, but he was a printer, working with inks at a press in Western New York. My story will not be complete without him, and I still miss him to this day. He will be interwoven in this story, because he saw so much of it.

The rail yards in Buffalo had activity, and served as the way station for grains from the midwest heading to the St Lawrence Seaway. They had employed three generations of my dad's family (his grandfather, his father, and my dad). The trains carried a wide variety of freight from the car plants in the North towns to other assembly plants in the area. Steel was, of course, one of the big loads. Then disaster struck. Conrail laid off a massive number of employees as competition from the trucking industry and the general economic downturn in the early 1980s affected the area. Dad was one of the firemen of Conrail who was bumped from his position. This was the fate of a lot of the Northeastern industrial zone in the US. In cities surrounding the Great Lakes, industry shuttered its doors, and the economy fell. Some economic historians claim that this was due to an economic retrenchment, as structurally, the economy adjusted itself to a loss of manufacturing jobs overseas. You can see the devastation wreaked in the economies all around western New York State. Buffalo as a city shrunk to half of its peak size. Niagara Falls, with the wonders of the cascading river over a major waterfall has, at least on the American side, become a city burdened with poverty. Jamestown and Dunkirk, once the northern and southern anchors of the Chautauqua county region, have lost industry and population. Devastation reached across the old Erie Canal boom area, as Rochester, Syracuse, Utica, and Schenectady lost the manufacturing spine that raised the economy and the wealth in the cities. Amsterdam, Johnstown, Gloversville, Elmira, Binghamton, and Olean became shrunken cities who in the 80s lost citizens, as they fled Upstate New York. The economy contracted as the state's upstate cities continue to hemorrhage industry and citizens.

For a bit of time there, my family relied on our relatives to help us out. One year for Christmas, we went over to my grandparents 20 acres in Elma to cut our tree. We got help as best we could for the little things. I ask myself, as I reflect on this fact, how did the American economy become broken? A man with a Bachelor's degree in Chemistry and a woman with a three year Diploma R.N. degree should have never been unemployed in the USA. I question the economic decision makers of the late 1970s and early 1980s. Why destroy the economy?

After some time of difficulty, my dad was offered a job working for the State of New York in Gloversville, NY. This change would lead us across the state and enter us into a new chapter of the family's existence.

REFLECTIONS:

- What are some of the earliest memories from your family?
- How does your family celebrate traditions? How can you help students learn about their family traditions?
- As a teacher, what are some unassumed traditions you have that your students may not?

[3]
CHANGES AND MOVEMENT

This chapter focuses on a radical shift for me, at an early age, and the significant loss in my life.

Guiding question: How have you dealt with loss/ change in your life?

BACKGROUND

This chapter begins to help you explain how a suburban kid became so interested in rural America. The differences between Buffalo and Gloversville were literally a state away. The dissonance of the two sides of the same state set foundations for later deep thinking during my PhD in education leadership, my teaching, and my service to the state and school improvement. Amazingly, with so many people so settled, not many people experience the dramatic differences between suburban and rural America, and the lack of understanding may be driving the cracks very apparent in American society. The juxtapositions are especially apparent in the lack of understanding of others between urban and rural America. A number of other writers have done a much better job exploring the phenomena, so please examine their work.

Our family packed up the house in Orchard Park and moved to the Adirondacks. My godfather, Steve, drove my dad's truck and the two dogs along with our outdoor stuff. My Mom and I were in the family car. Dad and Nick were in the U-haul. My Uncle Tom, who was working in Poughkeepsie for the State DOT as an engineer, met us. The new house would be an adventure for us, as we had a garage to explore and over 10 acres of land. The garage was packed with old machinery and wood. There was old farm equipment, made of metal, with gears and levers, sitting on a concrete slab, covered in dust and cobwebs. There was a second floor, filled with lumber of different types. Cherry wood and pine, smooth and cut at a mill. It was stacked in piles across the second floor, just waiting for two young boys to make believe they were building dinosaurs and creatures. The backlot of the house was a massive grass swath, over 10 acres, all available to run and hide in. Our favorite place was the underpass that connected the backyard with more land on the other side of State Highway 30a. It was like running into a tunnel that took you into another world, or between the ribs of a dinosaur like in a scene in a movie where the rib cage was sticking out of the ground.

My father, who received a Bachelor's in Chemistry from UB, had taken a civil service exam to work for the state of New York's Department of Environmental Conservation (DEC). This new job, totally different from the railroad, would move us to a small city on the edge of the Adirondack preserve. An hour west of Albany, Gloversville, NY was an old factory town that had lost its industry and a large chunk of its population in the 1980s as we moved there. My father would be working as a chemist, testing water from the Great Sacandaga Reservoir. He would be doing work to ensure the safety of citizens in the state, and the quality and purity of the lake that came to dominate the area.

Great Sacandaga was created as a way for New York State to alleviate the flooding which happened frequently downstream from the Black River District. This area that flooded so much was the capital district, just off the Hudson River. So the state created a major works project, flooding a large area of a quiet, tiny populated region. The lake stretches across multiple counties, and has created a large tourist attraction in the area. The lake submerged villages in the area, creating a vast area of emptiness. What was nice for us as kids was swimming in the lake, which my family often did. It was an easy drive from Gloversville to visit the numerous state parks in the area. The great forests of pine trees, planted as part of the environmental landscaping of the area, featured row upon row of tall, straight wooden posts, with natural trails between each row. There was a clean smell of pine, yes, but more importantly the smell of a lake, and the campfires and cooking fires in the park. The beach was a clean, crisp sand area, with a number of tall towers that the lifeguards would sit at and watch the swimmers. The picnic areas were small, secluded, and populated with tables that were well built, wooden, and a great place to have sandwiches. The park was a great place to spend a warm summer day as we relaxed and kept cool in the heat of July and August.

One of my other clearest memories of Gloversville was the State Department of Environmental Conservation lab. The lab had so many chemical glassware containers. There were beakers, and graduated cylinders, bunsen burners, and technology. It was, for a young boy interested in science, an amazing place. My dad's job was ensuring the test of water and air quality in the Adirondacks. In New York, the Adirondack State Park is one of the largest in the United States. He worked with a team checking on the health of the area. The Department of Environmental Conservation is charged with ensuring the health of New York State's environmental treasures.

The Adirondack Park is protected in the New York State Constitution as an area that needs to be kept forever wild. Earlier, the Adirondacks were logged, mined, and hunted before they were protected. The area is old geologically. It is home to what were once large seams of iron ore and large stands of old growth woods. The area is known for its plant and animal diversity. The area contains a number of lakes and rivers that are regarded as some of the best for canoeing in the US. Hikers who are looking to scale the peaks and become part of the "46ers" club seek out the Adirondacks high peaks, also known as the "46".

The Adirondacks are also home to Lake Placid, home of two US winter Olympics. The 1980 Winter Olympics is the most famous, as the "Miracle on Ice" happened when the US Men's Hockey team defeated the professional Soviet Union. The area is also home to the John Brown family farm, the final resting place for John Brown, who led the Harpers Ferry raid. The Adirondacks is bordered on the western range by the Fort Drum U.S. Army Base. The northern boundary of the park is the St. Lawrence Seaway and the Mohawk Nation. The south side rests against the Mohawk River Valley. Inside the park are a number of historical and recreational sites which included the hiking place that President Teddy Roosevelt was called from to assume the presidency when McKinley was assassinated in Buffalo, NY in 1904. Great Camp Sagamore is one of the old Gilded Age camps owned by the Vanderbilt family. Other sites in the Adirondacks include some of the oldest operating Boy Scout camps in the US, including Massawippi and Sabattis.

While we were in the Gloversville area, my mom worked as a member of the Littauer Hospital's nursing staff. In her role, she worked closely with the intensive care units. Mom's role on the nursing staff allowed her to help the people in Gloversville when they needed critical care. Many of the accidents in Gloversville were farm and industrial related. There were hunting accidents and auto accidents. The area around Gloversville was mountainous and hilly.

There was frequent fog and freezing rain. Another health care crisis in the area related to heart disease, stroke, diabetes, and alcoholism. The area had suffered a serious deindustrialization as the glove and clothing companies left for other parts of the world.

The area around Gloversville, part of the land granted to Sir William Johnson for his work with the Iroquois by King George II, holds historic Johnson Hall, built as a place to hold meetings and conduct trade events. The area is known for its Native American settlements by the Mohawk nation. Other historical sites in the area include the home of St. Kateri, one of the few North American Saints in the Catholic Church. Gloversville itself caters to people who are looking to travel into the Adirondacks for outdoor recreation. The area has seen increased demographic changes, as older eastern European immigrants moved out of the area and newer Latino families moved into the community.

One of our favorite activities when we were in Gloversville was getting ice cream in the area. As a family, we would go to Udderly Delicious and eat the ice cream. One the weekends, we would drive to Albany, NY to the recently opened Crossgates Mall and go shopping. We would also go out to eat in a family style. This was a great family day out in a larger community, more in line to what I remember in Buffalo. As a family, we would also attend Our Lady of Mt. Carmel. It was also where I went to school in 2nd grade. After a year in public school, my family decided I would do better in a private school.

In private school, we learned the religious foundations of our family's faith. School was marked by the rituals of the Catholic church and the secular teachings of school. Our class was fairly small, only about 18 students. We met as a class in an old school building, and the classroom from my memory was polished wood. As a class, we had a nice teacher, and one of our projects was to learn about the saint we were named after. Since my name is derived from Casmir, I had the opportunity to learn about St. Casimir, the king of Poland, and patron saint of Poland and youth. This sparked an interest in history, as I was able to use a really old textbook in the school's library to look up the information. I also gained a love for reading at home and in school, devouring books at the school and public library. My parents would take us to a bookstore in Albany, where we would buy books to take home. I love adventure stories and science fiction books. One of my favorite series was Encyclopedia Brown. As I read the series, I became enamored with the idea of solving problems. I enjoyed the amazing adventures of Encyclopedia Brown and friends looking for clues, and solving the problems of a small town. Falling in love with reading, a passion I continue to explore to this day, has helped me find facts and information, but has become an escapism which allowed me to venture on so many explorations that I would later in my life found to define me.

As a family, we also had one of our most difficult times in Gloversville. My family lost Adam, who was born with a number of medical issues. He needed oxygen from a tank, tubes connecting him to machines from the 1980s which are barbaric by 2010s standards. Mom taught us how to clean ourselves medically to hold Adam. She taught us how to feed him through his tubes. She taught us how to use the phlegm circular device to break up the packed mucus in Adam's one good lung. I remember visiting Adam in the Albany area hospital after he was born. I had to dress from head to toe in scrubs because I had a cold. I remember hearing the rapid beeping of the heart monitors on babies who were sick. I remember the smell of iodine in the Intensive Care Units for newborns. When we drove from Gloversville to Albany to visit Adam in the hospital, it was a long, cold and retching drive. My grandparents on both sides, my great aunts Charlotte and Terry, and Uncle Steve and Uncle Tom, would watch us as mom and dad would make the trek to stay with Adam. And then, after a Christmas time birth in 1982, Adam died near Easter, 1983. He needed another major surgery, and he was flown to Children's Hospital of Buffalo. But the surgery did not take. After four months on earth, my baby brother rejoined the angels of heaven. I have never seen my father cry before—racking- sobbing cries of despair. But I saw him—as he held my brother Nick and I in the living room of our house in Gloversville—the three boys of the Jakubowski family. Adam was gone. Our nuclear family was broken—and I still to this day— almost 35 years later weep at his gravestone in Buffalo, NY. He rests near his grandparents, his great aunts, uncles and cousins who have gone.

One area which struck me about Gloversville was the schools. Between the public elementary school and Our Lady of Mt Carmel Elementary, I only attended two years of elementary school in the area. What I remember about the school was a really different atmosphere than Orchard Park or Hamburg Elementary School. The students seemed different. The teachers were different. There was a feeling of impending doom in the elementary schools. Most likely this was caused by the lack of jobs in the area, but I could also see it in how I was treated as an outsider. I was really only accepted by the outsiders—Sarah who lived on a dairy farm and was a half a head taller than everyone else in 2nd grade and Chad—my friend who was an Army child. Almost all of the other kids were friends, and many were cousins. Their families had lived in the area since the gloving mills and textile plants had brought jobs to the area. These two years were my real introduction to rural life. Later, a career would emerge that would focus on the rural—as does my academic research.

REFLECTIONS:

- How do you deal with tragedy and trauma?
- How do major changes in the form of life altering events impact you and your work?
- How can you assist students/ colleagues/others who are dealing with major tragedy?

[4]
ADJUSTING AND REORIENTATION

This chapter focuses on a crucial moment in any family: recovery. How do you experience these moments? How do you recover? How do you find your center calling? The changes in our life make us who we are. They also create color.

Guiding question: How do you explain your movement into your "early independence" and how does that impact you as a teacher?

BACKGROUND

In 1983, my sister Emily was born, a miracle baby added to our family. We moved back to Buffalo, to be closer to family, and to have the support of friends and loved ones. Dad took a job as an industrial hygienist with the State Asbestos control department. Mom became a school nurse at Baker Victory services. Both jobs reflected the past, and present of Buffalo. During the age of industry, Buffalo constructed its manufacturing plants, houses, stores and schools with asbestos. A fibrous mineral, asbestos was great for containing heat. But it caused cancer in people's lungs when they would inhale the fibers. Dad was responsible for monitoring the contractors who were hired to remove and safely dispose of asbestos. It was a difficult job, especially in light of the money involved in the contractor's worlds. Dad, a servant leader, believed that it was a duty and an obligation to ensure public safety.

Mom worked with troubled youth at Baker Victory services, an outgrowth of the Venerable Nelson Baker charity work. Father Baker built a place for troubled and abandoned youth of unwed mothers. The institute later evolved into a place for youth with severe illnesses that challenged their mental and social capacity. Father Baker also constructed the Our Lady of Victory Basilica, a wonderment of the Lackawanna, NY skyline. Its dominant domes can be seen for miles around. But the church had secondary to the mission, helping children that others cannot or will not. My mom, an angel here on earth, took her nursing degree and her compassion and will to ensure all are protected to that place of hope and despair.

While my parents were doing the work of serving the community, in elementary school, my brother and I were trying to fit in. Having not grown up in the area, it was kind of hard to make friends. The kids at my school were nice—some of them—but others were real bullies. This was the age before bullying was a huge issue in school. After all —why not be tough and fight? That was the way of the suburban school. I do have to say though that I met an amazing teacher in my elementary years, Mrs. Sullivan. She cared so deeply for us. She gave creative lessons. She was an outstanding teacher who allowed growth in her classroom. Thank you Mrs. Sullivan for teaching us science, but also caring for us. If it weren't for her in fourth grade, I probably would have been nothing.

By the end of fourth grade, I needed friends, so my parents enrolled me in Cub Scouts. This is one of the most defining moments of my life. Without the scouting program, I do not know where I would be. The program gave me so much as I traveled in my journey to adulthood. What was even better was having my dad and my mom involved; dad became a den leader and then Cub Pack leader. Mom provided us with first aid training. I also met a good friend in Mark Zalikowski. A year younger than me, Mark was a computer guy who put up with me. I also became friends with Rick Schause. Rick had some medical issues from when he was younger. But we bonded over Star Trek. After a little bit, Rob Carnevale also befriended me. He was new to the area, but had a cool vibe about him. Such a group. By the end of elementary school, we were tossed into Junior high—a 7-9th grade monstrosity that took sixth grade students who were big fish in small ponds and made them little fish in a huge pond. I continued in scouts and became a Den Chief, working with my dad and my brother's Webelos den. In the summer of 1988, I went to camp Scouthaven near the village of Arcade, NY. Camp Scouthaven was an old railroad depot, with the dining hall having been the dance hall at the turn of the 19th to the early 20th century. We got lost, and were late (days before GPS). When you arrived at camp, your troop was checked in by the medical officer, sent through swim tests, and then toured the camps. I had an amazing time at camp, earning a number of ranks, skill awards, and Fishing Merit Badge. What I did not know was that back home my brother Nick missed me, so my grandfather took him to a farm and helped him get a pet, a Rabbit named Quicky. After losing Indie and Scottie in Gloversville, our family started to have pets again. My dad loved the rabbit—for its manure in his vegetable garden and the trees he planted.

In school I realized that there were some great teachers and some really mean ones. In 7th grade I saw a math teacher who would issue detention after two assignments were missed. The French teacher was a little batty- always talking with the popular kids. I don't remember much, but I do remember failing French in quarters 3 and 4 with a grade below 65. Yikes! Je ne parlez Francis bien, nes pas? I do remember my 7th grade social studies teacher—-Mr. Dyl—-a Civil War reenactor and a scouter. Mr. Dyl inspired us to learn history and engaged our class in the past by understanding and debating some of the ideas of history. Seventh grade made me realize that I liked history as a topic, and made me want to understand it deeper. Science held a deep pull on me as well. We went to Disney World and saw the science experiments of the hydroponic gardens. The idea of growing plants indoors was so new and so amazing to me. I realize that my mom and dad instilled a love of science in me due to the trips to Chicago to see the science center and the U-505 exhibit, the trips to Utah to see the promontory pointe historic park and the Dinosaur national monument. Family vacations—almost always tied to dad or mom's training for work—-were adventures of museums and book stores.

Eighth grade cemented my love of history, as Mr. James brought World War II alive in the classroom. I met Mrs. Waz that year- a math teacher who was also Jr. High Student government advisor. We bonded over my love of politics and government. She encouraged me to get involved with student government. I mostly remember the half birthday candy bars she gave to students with summer birthdays. The number of family pets grew as mom found and brought home a stray cat who we named Snowy because she was found in a snow storm. Snowy did not snuggle. She was her own cat. Between her and the rabbit- there was an uneasy truce. That was also a year I learned disappointment. During finals, some of the students misbehaved, so we all had to stay in the hot sweltering classrooms in June for the entire 3 hours allotted for exams. Because of where the junior high school was located, the downtown (village) location caused temptations for many students- especially with the new McDonald's which was built in the area. Students at the junior high school misbehaved so even the good students, like me, had to suffer. Another summer at camp—and I began to realize that I was in Scouts for life. I also realized I wanted to work summer camps. Since I was too young to work at Schoellkopf, I instead went to the YMCA of Greater Buffalo that summer- and I enjoyed the one week Counselor in Training job so much that I wanted to come back for the entire summer. I wound up working at the Y all of the summer of 1991. Here I met great people. I loved the handicraft section of the camp. I enjoyed the interaction.

As I transitioned into ninth grade, I met one of the most important people I have had the privilege of meeting. Mr. Mike Karpie, my business teacher and Distributive Education Clubs of America (DECA) adviser, would have a profound impact on me and my trajectory. I enrolled in Vehicle and Petroleum Marketing for competition. Karpie needed someone, and I wanted a chance. In January 1992, I won a top ten place award in the Western NY regions after taking a test and performing two role plays. I was hooked. I then went with Karpie and a number of people (Luke Goble, Jen McDowell, Jon Cervonie, Mark Szarowicz and others) to the old "Borscht Belt" hotels in Sullivan County. We stayed at the Concorde. Talk about impressive—gloved waiters. Soup and salad courses that were fancy. Amazing and splendid hotel spaces. Little did we know that the hotel would be torn down after we left. DECA Hamburg had a tradition of playing IRON MAN by Ozzy Osbourne as we pulled into the hotel on the bus. I met the Duffets, the Kuhns, and other leaders of the Hamburg business community on these trips. I met a number of awesome people at the state convention, but I learned to hate our bitter rivals from Long Island. Syosset, Half Hollow Hills, Walt Whitman, Commack—the names still ring in my dreams. They claimed a ton of spots, but so did Hamburg. And I won at states- for top test, and for Honorable mention (5th place). I just missed going to nationals DECA on my first trip! Mike Karpie really helped me turn my test taking and role playing abilities into a strength I still use today. I wished I had realized as a 14-15 year old how useful those skills were!

In 1993, I had a great year traveling and learning about leadership and service. The Greater Niagara Frontier Council sent me to Philmont for the National Junior Leader Instructor Camp at the beginning of the summer season. There I learned skills and techniques to successfully run a council level JLT course as a Senior Patrol leader. One of the greatest parts of being a member of the Abrau troop was the other scouts from around the US. A critical and important fact I learned about myself was how much sleep I needed to fully function. The hot dryness of Philmont showed me how beautiful the west was. That part of the world, parched as it is, has some inspiration for the soul. When I looked up in the night sky, I could see the vastness of the stars. I could feel the warm wind move along the mountains. For me the achievement of hiking up the Tooth of Time is one adventure that many scouts wish they had, and I got to experience the formation beyond the pictures in Boys Life, or other books about Philmont. As we were learning about teamwork, and dedication, and commitment to goals, I found out I had one more goal I wanted to fulfill.

In DECA, 1994 was my first year going to nationals. There I was recognized for achieving proficiency on all of the competition activities. What I loved most of all about nationals was the wide range of people who were out there. At Philmont, the Jambo, and at National DECA, I began to feel for the first time the weight of depression concerning my social failures subside. There were people out there who were like me. I just needed to find them! National DECA had some amazing opportunities at professional development. I began to practice networking, and ran into a number of people who from their feedback told me I could do something good for the world. It was nice to hear others talk to me in a positive way!

Teaching became one of my career pursuits in high school. As I had worked at the Y and Scout Summer camp, I became more and more interested in teaching. I joined the Future Teachers of America, and visited elementary classrooms. But my true passion was working with older students. I was finding myself asking teachers about how they became interested in teaching. I was enamored by presenting in front of a classroom. What I didn't realize was how hard it was. When one of my regular teachers went out on emergency leave, Mrs. Krolikowski, our public affairs teacher, allowed me to teach a class one day. It was hard. I also became interested in the idea of a doctorate in education. Dr. Duffner, my 10th grade social studies teacher, had completed a PhD at the University at Buffalo. He was an awesome teacher. Dr. Duffner used humor and visuals, and storytelling to make the history classes come alive, especially the 10th grade Global history class. He made the end of the year Regents exam seem as if it was just a rite of passage, not a huge hurdle for us. Mrs. K and Dr. D. were two of my favorite high school teachers who cared so much about their students.

I also learned compassion from Mrs. Cichocki, my math teacher. She was passionate, but also gave a break to a struggling student when math didn't work out for me. Mr Bill Gross taught me to be an actor when teaching, and Mr. Cammaratta, his student teacher, made Fredonia my school of choice.

The last and final highlight of high school was spring 1995. I earned Eagle Scout in 1993 so I continued with service in scouting. As such I undertook an environmental project for which I was awarded the Hornaday badge from the Scouts, for outstanding service in Conservation. At national DECA, I was recognized with a top test performance score nationally. I received a thick letter in the mail and had been accepted to SUNY College at Fredonia. Not only that, I was accepted into the Honors Department. The summer of 1995 would be my last at Scout Camp for a bit. I was getting ready for Fredonia and a new adventure! When we graduated that June of 1995, it was a great end and a great beginning. The class of 1995 would scatter around the United States. Some of us became educators, others moved into medicine. A number went on to serve our country in the military. We are and continue to do great things as a class.

REFLECTIONS:

- What are some influences from your high school experience that moved you to pick your profession?
- Select a mentor from your high school days. How did your mentor help shape you and your career journey?
- What can you do in your current role to help people make a positive change on their journey? What will you need to do to plan out this process?

[5]
TEENAGERS CAN BE CRUEL

I was bullied. There I said it. People I went to school with, who shall not be named, were really not nice. I was bullied for my weight, for my differences, and for my speech. I was bullied as a daydreamer, and considered odd. I was often alone at lunch, because the bullying hurt. It tore a hole in my soul. And what is worse, I hated that others were bullied too.

Like a cliche of a movie, the bullying did not end until I played sports in high school. Once I put on the ceremonial jersey of a football player in 10th grade, and went onto the field, I was accepted.

We must change society. We must end the shark attacks on victims who had no fault. I see so much talent waste or MUDA in the world, and I see so much bullying. The talent waste emerges as the person subjected to the bullying retreats, and disengages. A scientist is destroyed, a kindergarten teacher never emerges, a lawyer cannot win that case to punish a major polluter. These repercussions are costing the United States millions of dollars as students quit toxic environments in their schools. Even as the state and federal government have mandated anti-bullying, there is still way too much non engagement. And the situation is even worse in the workforce. I will give an example in a later chapter. In my opinion, there are four types of bullies, who operate in many ways unchecked in the world. Kristen Hadeed, in Permission to Screw Up (2007, Penguin) tells a story about how a bully destroyed, for the moment, her company. Bullies continue to wreck schools, workplaces, and our nations. The four types are: unaware, unwise, outlashing, and outcasts. Why these four types? Well let me explain.

Four Types of Bullies

UNAWARE

An unaware bully is unaware of how their interactions are causing pain. They may not "get it" because their brains have not grown to maturity. The unaware bullies may be committing what we adults call microaggressions, or unintentional attacks on someone for a characteristic or behavior that causes harm. An unaware bully may have no idea what is happening due to their perception of the world around them and their limited world view. They may say "wow you're fat" to a heavy person, because they are immature, or the bully is experiencing these stimuli for the first time and has no idea how they should react, because they are unaware of people who are overweight. It's an almost childlike state which requires people to educate the bully that really, they are being harmful.

An unaware bully has a worldview problem. They are very self-centered. They may have been an only child, or may have an issue with how they relate to others. My dearest, most valued colleague of all time, Nancy Hinkley, had to help me once in a class we co-taught. Two very able students were saying really uncool things about different ability students. These two students had privilege, and had positionality, but demanded to know why the other students received accommodations, and how NOT FAIR that was. So Nancy completed the MOST POWERFUL LESSON I HAVE EVER SEEN!

What Nancy did was really amazing. She worked the two students through a series of exercises that created a similar sensory input experience which students with those diagnosed issues lived with. There was one exercise in which the student needed to draw a star in a mirror, to create the reality of a student trying to learn atypically. A second exercise created for neuro-typical students the experience of dyslexia. After three attempts, one of the young men expressed his deep and profound apologies for the way in which he had so dismissively and contemptuously thought about the accommodations others received in class.

In summary, unaware bullies are people who are truthfully unaware that what they are doing is creating harm. The individual, or the group, does not understand the impact their words, deeds or actions have on the victim. Their own blindspot and lack of education is the biggest impediment to personal growth. A well designed and executed education program, with early intervention should make a profound difference in this individual's or group's path, and potentially end the bullying early, and in the end, create an anti-bullying advocate.

UNWISE

An unwise bully is slightly different than an unaware bully. An unwise bully knows, somewhere, that what they are doing isn't quite right.Their actions toward their victim shades towards mischief. They usually want to do something that will gain social status with their "in crowd" because the action, or word, or activity is perceived as edgy or dangerous, or establishes a "power" imbalance with the victim. Some example behavior include passive-agressive comments towards an obese student: "Do you really need that dessert?" Other unwise bullying activities can be pointing out how someone is wearing the same clothes again, in order to embarrass the other person. An unwise bully may also start rumors not for malicious reasons, but because there is an element of "fun" among the "popular" group. Examples of unwise bullying behavior include athletes exerting social dominance within a school, or creating a "no go zone" in the cafeteria. The unwise bully type engages in a realization later in life that, indeed, they made mistakes, and takes responsibility. They will often outreach, or apologize at formal gatherings in the future.

OUTLASHING

Whereas the unaware and the unwise bullies may have limited fault for not truly understanding the implications or the impact of their actions, an outlashing bully suffers from an awareness of what is happening, and has a deeper and more troubling explanation. An outlashing bully is usually the victim of bullying in their own life. They may be suffering mental, emotional, physical, or sexual trauma and are lashing out at others in order to gain some inner peace. An outlashing bully is trying to recapture some semblance of control over their own life by inflicting harm on others. The outlashing bully may have two central focuses. The first focus victim emerges from those people who are unable to stand up for themselves. The outlashing bully victimizes the perceived weaker or less socially adept persons in their ecosystem. The outlashing bully inflicts damage on the victim to gain a modicum of relief, and to prove to their own psyche that there is some modicum of value, because the bully can force their will on someone else.

The second type of victim of the outlashing bully is their tormentors. The outlash occurs when the bullied person engages in a fight with, or actions against the perpetrators of their own angst. This type of victimization is popular in revenge sequences in films, such as the *Karate Kid* or *A Christmas Story*. In both stories, the bullying victim seeks revenge against the aggressor and wins, usually after humiliation in previous sequences. In both instances in the movie, this type of outlash bullying is celebrated as standing up for one's self.

In masculinity, and for many years culturally, a person who was the victim of an aggressor was treated like a defective person, until they could prove the ability to "stand up for themselves" without an external authority intervening.

An outlashing bully may be profoundly impacted, and in many ways may be a victim. This is especially true in school systems which have refused to acknowledge that there is bullying at the unaware, and unwise levels among their students and staff. When an outlashing bully finally receives help, they often understand that their inner rage was in response to feelings of helplessness, and often feel remorse. The difference between an outlashing bully and an outcast is more profound, and disturbing.

OUTCAST

The toughest of the four types of bullies in my opinion, an outcast bully is bordering on truly dangerous, and extremely unstable. An outcast bully intentionally knows what rules and social norms are broken in the act. The group or individual plots to actively hurt a person, or another group in order to gain some sort of gratification. Unlike the unaware or outlashing bully, the outcast bully suffers no gaps of information or no internal pain. The outcast is different than the unwise, who knows what is doing, but believes it to be in a fun fashion, or a legitimate purpose. An outcast bully needs significant help. This individual may have suffered in the past, and is outlashing, but not to protect themselves or as a cry for help. The outcast intends to inflict damage, make someone suffer, and gain a reputation as a malcontent. In my opinion, this type of bully graduates to socio and psycho-path level danger and damage to themselves, the school, the environment, and the community. Whereas an outlashing bully may be trying to settle a score, the outcast is trying to score points in some way, shape or form. They want to intimidate, and create chaos, all so they are not accountable to the system or to community values.

PERSONAL AND PROFESSIONAL IMPACT

So what has been the impact on my life because of what I experienced in school and life? For starters, I often perceive myself as an impostor. I never really quite believed I belonged. I have also found myself hypersensitive to injustices, perceived and real. I am especially vigilant to the ways in which people who do not have power are impacted by what I perceive as bullying behavior. I become quite emotional at seeing pain, or sadness. I find myself often trying to rescue people.

Professionally, I find myself frequently disappointed by people who are in power and authority positions when actions do not result in positive outcomes for those in their charge. In other words, I want to right wrongs, correct injustices, and fight for the oppressed. Except that does not work in the real world. Compromise is the name of the game, and I find myself frequently annoyed that the ideal is unachievable.

REFLECTIONS:

- What in your career is a "bright line" that you feel needs changing?
- Of the four bully types, what are some ways you can identify and enact changes in your school to prevent their spread?

[6]
FREDONIA AND COLLEGE

We never arrive at college forgetting who we are. College is a transformational experience. For many of us, we were so lost. How did your experiences change you? I relate the story of my college days, and my evolution from learner into a teacher.

Guiding question: What do you know now you really wish you could tell your younger self?

BACKGROUND

Going to college and residing away from home has always been a memory I will cherish as I think about the professors, classmates, and experiences I held. I entered as a Social Studies 7-12 major, and quickly added a second history major. During orientation, I first realized I was a stuffed sack, and had tried to loosen up. Unfortunately, for me I still could not shake the bullying I had undergone at school to see I didn't need to be a starched and rigid person. I really wish I could have relaxed. I really wish I had learned how to enjoy it. My first year at Fredonia was amazing: meeting Tom Morrissey who was an artist as a teacher and a scholar of repute. His lectures were funny, engaging and did a ton to introduce us to the Western Civilization that we were exploring. Tom is one of those teachers you just need to follow and take classes with no matter what time of the day. I also met Dr. Laurie Buonanno, in Political Science. I love political science, and use its structures to describe my research now on rural schools. She would be a mentor, and every chance I had, I would take a class with Laurie. One regret I have is not staying in school for an extra semester and earning a Poli Sci minor. So close. Sigh.

That first year I took an honors seminar with Greg Adams. The class was full of high achievers who were interested in adolescents and their problems and transitions. It was intensive and interesting. Ted Steinburg, the leader of the program, held us all in a colloquium or discussion section. This was so intellectually stimulating and interesting to me. I loved meeting and chatting with everyone in the program. Such freedom, such discussion. The sociology class I took that first semester introduced me to identity and to class, and power. It was fascinating, and made such a difference in how I viewed the world. My second semester on campus was a mess. I did ok, but the death of my grandmother on my mom's side, and the death of my grandfather on my dad's side messed me up. I also had trouble in the coaching classes I took. Just didn't seem to get along with the coaches (because I hated sports and really didn't understand why social studies teachers needed to take coaching). My two honor classes that semester were really high level. Human Reproductive Biology examined processes of how the DNA and RNA work. The second honors course was Comedy and Humor in Literature taught by Dr. Mac Nelson. He was a hoot- from the English Department. He made humor come alive, from the works of Shakespeare to the academic tropes of David Lodge's *Changing Places*. We read *Life at*

Blandings and a series of other humor and comedy books. When I met with him to discuss my paper for the class, he told me, with a smirk and a forbearance that I still remember almost 20 years later, "Casey, I see you surrounded by books...." he became so right on so many levels.

The spring semester started with me going back to Hamburg and observing my teacher Dr. Duffner for a week. We needed to gain 30 hours of field observation and report on it. I remember watching him teach, and watching the class. It was an odd experience to eat in the teacher's cafeteria, and visit the lounge. My home high school felt different, even if I had just been there less than a year ago. Now I wore a tie, instead of a sweatshirt or a sweater. I also saw my teachers in a different light. They talked about much more than their subjects. They actually interacted. They read the newspaper and discussed sports and vacation and their own kids. A peek behind the curtain was so flooring to me. This was going to be my life, and I had to get used to it.

Student government at Fredonia allowed me to meet people who had a fairly good mind, but here again, I wish I had rethought this action. I liked parliamentary procedure,and when I went to a Student Association meeting with a group I had belonged to, I saw how poorly run the organization was and wanted to help. So midway through, I was the Parliamentarian. My job kept meetings running, and ensured that procedure was followed by members and groups. It had just enough service, but no need to run for office. I liked it. That summer, I did not work at Scout camp for the first time in 5 years. Instead, I worked in landscaping. That job taught me that hard working, physical laborers do not get enough credit for what they do. I cut lawns, I changed out bushes and shrubs, I installed fences. I replaced drainage tile, and I installed lawns from rolled turf. I even painted doors. It was decent money but I learned how hard it is to make money. Especially when the weather didn't cooperate and we couldn't work for the day. My boss was really scattershot, and didn't do well with running a small business. This sparked a desire in me to understand how to help small businesses.

When I returned to campus that fall, I became a TA for Dr. Laurie Buonanno and tutored in the Learning Center. I took a really cool honors seminar by Dr. Hurtgen where I read a lot about civics and civic engagement in the community. This one book, called *Habits of the Heart* by Bellah, et al. (HarperCollins, 1985) made a huge impact on me. The book described how individualistic American society in 1985 was, and how we were breaking apart at the seams. The book described in some detail how people had stopped socializing, caring for neighbors, and became islands unto themselves. This class enabled me to see how significant a community and the people in a community are to each other. It also resonated with me as an historian and now as an educational researcher studying rural schools.

I was also introduced to Dr. A.J. Swansinger, an amazing professor who knew a ton about a lot. She inspired my craving for knowledge about world history, and how to better teach it. She also taught me to not just research but to write. We collaborated that semester on a departmental project to help advise students in history and social studies. Jackie is to this day one of the most feared, respected, and revered professors at Fredonia.

That spring, I loaded up on classes. I had determined I was going to graduate early. It was a heavy semester, where I was in multiple history classes and working on the required historiography class. This class teaches students what the story of history is. There is no cannon. There are interpretations and speculations, and sources marshalled into an argument which can be accepted or rejected by different people for different reasons. We studied the decision to drop the atom bomb. There were a ton of books to read and a ton of papers to write. I was also tired. It had been a tough year trying to do so much. Volunteer efforts and clubs began to give way to readying for student teaching and my career. I did like the classes on world political geography and the Middle Ages classes, again taught by my favorite professors, Dr. Thomas Morrissey. Scott Van Alstine, who to this day is one of my dearest friends, studied and hung out. We were acquaintances with people who would go on to be border agents, lawyers, teachers, and solid middle of the road folks. Most of us became part of greater machines, and didn't really stand out. We landed, and softly, but not to the level we thought. In reflection, we weren't networked into the colleges that would have propelled us into leadership positions. This is an odd reflection, as our youth leadership training as Eagle Scouts (three out of five) for roles destined to improve the world.

That spring also introduced me to an abhorrent and mutant part of education which caused me consternation, as I was shocked by what I saw at a field placement. I am calling myself out for my positionality, that I am middle class, white, male, cisgendered, and come from a privileged position of an intact nuclear family. What I witnessed in the course of my semester at the field placement made me cringe. First, I needed a car to commute from Fredonia to Cassadaga. Seven miles away from SUNY Fredonia, a paradigm of higher learning was an ill fated attempt at helping at-risk folks succeed. I witnessed little teaching or learning at the location (not a traditional school). There was chaos. There was test prep. Each day, the teacher would break out packets of test preps from previous GED tests. The students would then try to answer the questions in the test prep and hand it in to the teacher to grade. After marking the incorrect answers wrong, they would hand the test prep questions back and the students would do it again. Really, I remember one student who did this 5 times with a 4 answer multiple-choice question test. The stories that the students had to share were heartbreaking. Most were from New York City. Most had suffered a trauma in their life—a family member killed, a child born before 18, a serious illness in the family. Many were recent immigrants to the United States. Their home schools were no help—many students had dropped out, and wanted to take advantage of a second chance opportunity via this program. It wasn't public. It was operated by the lowest bidding private company that wanted to make a profit on the backs of the teachers and the students. Teacher turnover was really high. Counseling services weren't meeting the student/clients needs. It is a classic example of how a for-profit corporation with little oversight can do some really shady things. Nothing illegal, but morally questionable.

That summer I worked retail. My job was to help in the lawn and garden- seasonal. This meant helping people with mulch and tools, soil, and plants. It was hard work, and I felt weird in the big box. It paid nice, for a college kid with supportive parents, and I liked having cash in hand. I also took a class at college in Native American history. It was inspiring, depressing and informative all at the same time. Native Americans are here, and the Native communities are a font of wealth and expertise, and survivors. The work of the Mohawk people in high steel is inspirational! The leadership of people who became subject to lies and manipulation really demonstrates an abusive history by the nation. And with so many controversies surrounding how to teach history, the "Whig version" of the US can do no wrong, or the attempt at discovering the past warts and all, rages. It is scary to see how much brainwashing exists in American schools. There are some real issues folks. We must do better!

I discovered some real abuses in corporate America, when workers are not protected from exploitation. The Assistant Store manager had us change her tires or add a flat. We were often told to watch, and cut our hours, as the store went over budget. We were directed to sell, even without a commission. Our training videos told us unions were bad, and our job was to prevent theft or shrinkage. We were instructed to look out for others who may be stealing and report them immediately. The store used to lock in workers for the night to assemble the chairs, mowers and other products for customers. Often it was easier to buy lunch at the store than to attempt to go someplace else.

Fall of 1997 was my last on campus. I lived in an apartment off campus starting my sophomore year, and again my junior year (fall 1997). That year I took most of my education classes. I remember having met Dr. Maheady and Dr. Malette. They were two dynamic duos of the educational faculty, educators who cared about students and cared about schools. Both focused on the special education students. The two instructors wanted us to focus on scaffolding teaching for students. Help the students help themselves. Make sure the students know they are supported.

My teaching methods course was that semester as well. To this day, I still feel like I learned very little about good teaching practice. Come to find out, our professor was on a terminal appointment. They had not earned tenure and were basically searching for a new position. That semester was the time when the college was attempting to help us in the job search process. And I picked a real doozy. Social Studies teachers are a penny a hundred (dime is too high). There was a bit of a glut on the market. We were told so at practice interviews which were set up for us that semester. I also later found out that many New York State trained teachers move out of state, to signing bonuses and welcoming arms in the south and west. As I was wrapping up life on campus, and my undergraduate career, I also put in for field placement.

For many teachers (and there is a ton of research, see Miller in the *Journal of Research in Rural Education*), finding the siren song of home (within 50 miles) ideal for their leap into a career. PLEASE resist the urge and go away! You must see how other parts of the state do things differently! Student teaching is the AAA level practicum. We are not, however, paid for our efforts (I have a chapter in my book, *Thinking About Teaching*, where I ponder the equity of this practice). For all of our work, many field placement supervisors get a little extra— free tuition voucher, or a flat amount of money. For many veteran teachers, there had been a sort of underground trading market, where they would sell vouchers for cash to their colleagues who needed graduate credits. New York at this time required teachers to earn a master's degree, and those are expensive. The vouchers then were a lifeline for teachers making a good "salary" for everyday folks, but not enough to keep body and soul together. Teaching, especially at the earliest ranks,is one of the most underpaid professions in the US (Please see research by literally anyone).

Spring semester (1998) meant a move back home and student teaching. One placement assigned me to teach middle school social studies for grade 7 at the cross town rivals. The second placement would be with my Economics teacher at my high school. Trying to have student teachers at different levels is good for professional growth. You can see the difference developmentally between a middle school student in grade 7, and a high school senior who has just turned 18. You notice a lot about learning styles, content retention, and personality. Classroom management and lesson structure are fundamentally the same, but have very different nuances—almost like a banker who deals with personal finance and a different one who sells to businesses. One thing is for certain, a semester student teaching is not enough to get you ready for the rigors of the profession.

As I started my seventh grade placement, I found that my cooperating teacher did not believe in a lot of the "new fangled stuff." In fact she rejected cooperative learning activities and student-driven learning. To her, a good lesson started with the students reading the text the night before and filling out a worksheet outline which listed the names, dates, and major vocabulary from the lesson. She would then spend the first 10 minutes of class going around the room and checking in the outlines. Then she would give a quiz for five minutes about two people or events or concepts from the reading before. The kids would trade papers and then tell her the scores which she would mark into a grade book. She then spent the last 30 minutes of class going over the notes from the section last night. Slowly, deliberately, repeatedly. It was funny to watch her in the teacher's lounge. She really disliked one of her classes. She also felt professional development was a waste of time, and believed that the school wasted her time as a professional. At grade team meetings, she would often talk about how badly some of the students were doing. Often a "frequent flyer" or student who was known to all for classroom management infractions would earn a detention or a note home.

When I asked her about why she taught history, she told me (paraphrasing here): Oh, it was easier than math. I really liked math, but history was so much easier. She also would never leave the classroom, and would often stop and correct me in the middle of a lesson, in front of the students. What was worse was a lesson I taught about the Revolutionary War—where I created mini bags for groups to explore and Hardtack for them to eat. I included in those bags items that were close proximities to what a Revolutionary soldier would carry in their bag. The idea was to help students understand the weight of the items, and their impact on life. She told me the lesson was really underdeveloped and poorly executed. My field supervisor from Fredonia loved it. That was massive cognitive dissonance! Granted I admit I could have done better, but really, I put a ton of effort into the lesson.

I also became really sick during my last week of student teaching with strep throat. Note to all people who are interested—teaching is a Germ Warfare profession! Take care of yourself! I was running a 102 fever and coughing. That meant she needed to plan the lessons and was a bit peeved. So when time came to be evaluated, she gave me mediocre marks.

My next placement at my home school district with my old Econ teacher was much better. I stuck to the script and followed his lead. It was great to see my old teachers again and to talk with them about the highs and lows of the profession. My cooperative teacher was very supportive, gave me plenty of freedom, and allowed me to introduce new ideas into the classroom. It was nice to see the students react positively to the class and to the work which we did together. I really wished I could have taught at home. But it was not meant to be. At the end of the school year, I found myself subbing for my home district, which for many teachers is the pathway into the profession. And subs get paid crazy low amounts! No benefits, and as of this writing $100 a day. It may seem like a lot, and would be if it was guaranteed, but it is not. You are often called at the last minute with little support from the school.

REFLECTIONS:

- What are some of your memories from your college days?
- How can you examine your students' experiences from over their summer sessions to inspire a new year?
- What role do pets play in our lives? How does pet care demonstrate connections with academics in school?

[7]
FIRST TEACHING JOB

The follies of youth! I reflect on my first teaching job and the hidden curriculum. How little did I really know? Fair warning, take a look at my book *Thinking About Teaching* (2020) for some background....

Guiding question: What from your first teaching job did you take away? What do you wish you could get from your first job? What is your dream first job?

My first teaching job was in the enchanted mountains of Cattaraugus County, NY. The area is home to some of the greenest, and natural areas in New York. The first impression you have as you stare south as you begin the slow climb up the foothills while traveling on Route 219 is the green peaks of the southern tier. If you stop and look to the north, you can see downtown Buffalo, Lake Erie, and even, on really clear days, the mist of Niagara Falls thrown into the air. Streams and rivers cut the mountains of the area deeply. The glaciation of the past epoch created deep grooves within the landscape that gave rise to the undulating flow of the landscape. Deep within those valleys, you can feel the echoes of the Native American nations who lived in the area. The Seneca nation has a reservation there, around the city of Salamanca. You can still see the impact of the railroads in the large Victorian homes that line main street. They sit quietly, some in good repair, others divided up into multiple apartments. There is a stately grandeur in those buildings. They have seen the good times and the bad—the boom and the bust. Moving along main street, you can see the poverty mixing with the middle class money in the form of small businesses that are trying so hard to survive in the southern tier.

One of the greatest attractions in Salamanca is the Native American Veterans Pow Wow. Held in the central park in the city, it is a kaleidoscope of Nations in their finery, a riot of sound and a cacophony of smells. In order to honor both the culture of the community, and to praise the military veterans, the Natives come together in a festival of dance, music, and food. This yearly event provides a wonderful, living look at the Iroquois nations, the other Native nations which join the festivities, and the solemn remembrance of the servicemen and women who never made it home. The drum circle called out the songs and rhythms of the dance were paired with the flutes and singing of artists who have given their hearts and souls to maintain the culture and customs of their people. Coupled with the dress and regalia of the dancers, there existed a mesmerizing effect on the audience. The blues, greens, reds and the sounds of the bells attached to the clothes flashed in an intricate pattern of life. When coupled with the smell of the frybread and the corn stew, you could almost forgive the touristy cotton candy. I, for one, appreciated the tastes and textures of the food the vendors sold. It added so much to the already amazing adventure of Salamanca.

In the old Salamanca mall sits a huge antiques world, where there is a ton of furniture, knick-knacks and the occasional treasure including military and baseball trading cards. This is a great place to be lost, as you smell the mustiness of the antiques mixed in with the metal oil from the clocks and sewing machines. The light playing off the glass lamps and crystal glasses in the curio cabinets amuses the eyes. The smell of wood polish reaches you from some of the old desks and bookshelves. The furniture on the floor are straight out of a museum, but are priced for the Toronto or Buffalo tourist looking for that object d'art to show the family has some culture, even if they didn't have any when that furniture was brand new. The craftsmanship is amazing to behold, and you see the efforts of the workers who labored to make the piece for the purchaser. The mall is located downtown, near an old hotel, and some other storefronts that hold the typical pizza shops and the Chinese takeout place that is actually quite good. Driving just outside the city, north to Ellicottville, south to Allegany State Park, the mountains and the river remind you that the area still retains some of the natural beauty that drew vacationers to the area for skiing and camping.

The Allegheny River that runs through the area breaks off Allegany State Park, a lovely area full of camping and natural beauty and the reservoir. It is the site of a massive fraud perpetrated against the Native American nations of New York State. Laurence Hauptman (*Iroquois Struggle for Survival*, Syracuse Press, 1986) does a wonderful job describing how New York took a reservation and flooded a large area of it in order to create the Allegheny Reservoir. That sad stain on the soul of the state is not the first, nor the last time the state and federal government has hurt native Americans.

The summer of 1998 was very stressful for me, a social studies teaching graduate. So many resumes and no job offers. I was working at a Scout Summer camp near Arcade, NY, 40 miles south of Buffalo, serving as the Outdoors Director. And I was interviewing. I left camp a lot in order to interview, and it wasn't until the end of the camp season in August when my boss asked his buddy, the Postmaster of a small community, to help me out. The postmaster was golfing buddies with the principal at a small K-12 district in the area. Networking is key.

Most jobs are found through knowing someone. Don't let your ethics get in the way of networking! You need to realize that sponsorship, or people advocating for others without power via networking, is a crucial strategy for making change.

The School District was, well, small! There were 280 kids in the entire district K-12. That is very small for New York, and considering I grew up in suburbia, with a graduating class of over 250 students. When I arrived on the campus for my interview, I was amazed at the age of the school. It was a Works Progress Administration building constructed in the late 1930s, just as the local one-room school houses had centralized into the School District. It had been expanded a bit over the years. The floor was polished and very wooden. The school was surrounded on all sides by other buildings. It had nowhere to expand. The local restaurants in the area were a chain sub shop in a gas station and a local diner/bar. And not much else. The teaching staff was small, with two teachers per elementary grade and two teachers per subject area in the secondary school. I was interviewing for a grade 7-12 social studies position with responsibilities to teach seventh grade, ninth grade, and split 11 and 12 grade social studies with the other teacher in the department. I was thrilled as I showed the interview committee my portfolio of works from undergraduate school. At the end of the interview the principal said something to the effect of the consolidation not affecting the position. I didn't really register what he said to me, because I, as an extrovert, loved the interview, and loved showing off my handiwork to people. So two days before my 21st birthday, the school district called and offered me a teaching position! I was excited. I was going to be a social studies teacher! I was moving to live in the community! I immediately started to plan for my classroom. I went to the University at Buffalo's library and started to photocopy journal articles on teaching social studies. I was going to make the year the best I could for the kids!

The principal of the school helped me get an apartment down in the area, in a tiny hamlet. It was a one bedroom apartment in an old farmhouse that had been converted into single bedroom apartments for four people. The landlord was a retired sheriff's deputy. The house was right next to massive farms. The area was amazingly scenic. It was the western side of the mountain from Holiday Valley ski resort in Ellicottville, NY, a major destination for Buffalonians and Canadians. The "Enchanted Mountains" of Cattaraugus county are just that. The fog and mists that rise from the valley at dawn shroud the valley in a thick blanket of dew and newness. I had more than once witnessed herds of deer climbing up and down the hills next to the highways.

As I moved in and got settled in the community, I had three days before school began. In New York, the school year starts right after Labor day. In 1998, Labor Day was late! It was September the 7th. That first week of September was spent moving to the area and getting into the classroom and going through orientation. When I went to school, I had a shock. The textbooks for my classes were beat up. And they were soft covered. Soft cover social studies textbooks are never a good idea. Most had chapters missing from them. I had graduated from a suburban school with a lot of supplies and materials. My new district had some, but not nearly enough for me. I called my former high school teachers and asked if there were any resources I could use for my classroom. He had some and provided me with some document books. I also asked the secretary for any budget money and bought some materials, but again, not nearly enough in my opinion. In education, our funding formulas are driven by pupil numbers, not really needs. So the bigger districts get the advantage of size, and small districts are left without.

It's not uncommon for first year teachers to go straight from college into difficult teaching assignments, be they rural or urban cities. In fact, a number of research studies suggest that new teachers wind up in difficult to staff schools facing difficulties (Miller& Youngs, 2021,). I was thrilled when I met a seasoned English teacher who was to mentor me as I went through my first year trials. After all, I had just graduated and knew a lot about the teaching theory and content for a social studies teacher. What I didn't realize was how difficult the year was going to be. After all, how could I? It was my first ever teaching job, and I was just slightly older than some of my students. In fact, one student was married and had a baby girl at home. This is the classic definition of an at-risk student. These students were white, mostly, and very much in poverty. The area was poor. After the deindustrialization of the region, and the declining resource extraction industry, the last thing this community needed was a collapse of farm prices. The farm prices for all sorts of goods, such as milk, produce and grains tanked. A tourist community, a ski town to the east has grown rapidly into a tourist destination, now thriving and becoming remarkable in its middle class and upper class-ness. A rather large steep mountain blocked the spill over. The hills and valleys in between may have limited interaction between the different communities throughout the region.

As the year opened, we as a faculty were treated to the usual beginning of the year festivities in a school district in the state. This meant sitting through new employee orientation and the staff training that makes up the gap week between August 31 and the new school year. Employee orientation for the new staff started with filling out paperwork: Authorization to work, emergency contact, joining the state retirement system, and the oath of office. I read the oath of office and it puzzled me. It asked me to swear that I had never been a member of a group intent on overthrowing the government, and that I supported the state and federal constitution. In my historian's brain, I wondered what the hell this was about? It wasn't until much later, studying for my Master's Degree in history that I realized these oaths were left over from the communist hunts of the McCarthy era (Heins, 2004).

The principal opened the welcome by telling us about his experience as a new teacher in that very district. The event happened during a time of enrollment crisis and certification changes, when he was new coming into the school while a number of other teachers were fired and made to leave. In New York State, teaching has become increasingly credentialed as the state and federal government have taken an increasing interest in the local doings of education. Tracy Steffes (2004), Nancy Beadie (2008) , and Benjamin Justice (2012) have all done a much better job describing the changes than I could in this work. In the beginning, local districts were on their own to certify teachers to teach in the state. The local District Superintendent, who was originally the overseer of all the little one-room school houses, would complete this task. Now, the State Education Department, in conjunction with colleges and universities, ensures we are all "highly qualified" to teach in our subject matters.

After the orientation, we were taken to see our classrooms and get them set up. The next day was the formal gathering of all staff members. Here we received the mandated right-to know training which covered safety for first aid, chemicals, and basic drills like a fire drill. Pre Columbine, schools didn't worry about potential disasters. The superintendent gave the address welcoming us to the school year. He addressed some changes the school made, including matching a potential merger partner's block schedule as we prepared for the progress of the potential merger. He welcomed the new staff, including the new music teacher, math teacher, the other social studies teacher, and me. The social studies department (of two) had a 100% turnover. Apparently, this was not the first year that such a thing had happened. After the superintendent's welcome, we had our meeting with the union leadership and a luncheon. This traditional first day approach to the school year has welcomed teachers to the realm of professional education for decades.

What I remember next was a meeting to divide up the extra chaperone duties for the year. I had no idea what this was about, and sat and listened as the more senior teachers took duty assignments. Apparently this was one way that teachers in rural schools make up for a lack of some base pay. They take extra duty assignments that allow for a small increase in income. This is especially important for the very senior teachers who are looking to retire. Most pay scales in rural districts are severely depressed compared to the pay scales of more urban and suburban regions of the state (Miller, 2012) .

As the first days of school began, I met the students for the first time. They were an eclectic group of students in this little rural village and the surrounding countryside. My teaching schedule was like no other I had encountered in my field experiences and student teaching. I was responsible for two sections of 7th grade, two sections of 9th grade, one section of 11th grade, and one section of Economics 12. I was also assigned a study hall. The classes were blocked, and only met every other day. The classes were 73 minutes in length, because that is what the school had adopted when there was discussion about merging with our next door neighbors. I could not believe how much free time I had, and yet how much the time was too short.

As I began to teach my students, some stood out. There was a married 12th grader with a baby. One of my students was the son of my landlord's girlfriend. Two of my students were children of the Board of Education members. Other students were the children of fellow teachers. One of my 12th graders had already graduated from basic training, and was waiting for his service in the army to begin after graduation. I had a few students who were repeaters from last year. In a small school, you fail a grade, and you have the same teacher again. In my case, I was replacing a teacher who had left for suburban Buffalo. Instead of the same teacher, they would have a new one.

As the fall progressed, the village came alive with the sights and sounds of the fairs and fests. The sports games were especially attractive. Almost the entire school community would turn out to watch the school play its rivals. Our team was mighty in heart, but lacking in strength and ability, and lost. Our varsity team was composed of 9-12 graders, just to keep the team with enough members to play against the other teams. Students asked each other out for homecoming. There was a major parade, and it seemed like everyone was there. All of this was set against the backdrop of a merger.

In 1958, New York State published a Master Plan to School District Reorganization. In an effort to make New York Schools more efficient, the legislature, with the State Education Department, had devised a plan to encourage districts to first centralize, and then consolidate. The centralization stage started with the state calling on Common Schools to combine into a school district which could offer K-12 education in their communities. The Common Schools, by law, could only offer schooling up to grade 8. After that, students needed to attend a school or an academy to earn a high school diploma. Remember, for a long time period most people did not obtain a high school diploma. In fact, New York State has had for almost 200 years a series of exams at the end of the year called Regent's Exams in order to certify students as ready for college. The idea of graduating from high school has only taken off since 1983. Now, in 2016, students and schools are required to complete high school and earn a diploma in the state. In many of the more rural communities, the first time a local high school emerged occurred when the local Common Schools were centralized into a Central School District. The District was created by the state in order to educate the children in the village and some of the surrounding communities. The state was not done there, however. New York's Master plan for school reorganization called for Little Valley to join with a larger neighboring Central School district, eight miles away. Time and again between the birth of the district and when I joined the staff in 1998, the community was subject to consolidation studies with every neighbor multiple times. The district had not merged, and was alone in its attempts to educate the valley students.

The expansions the physical Works Progress administration building had undergone had resulted in more classroom space, but the building was landlocked in the village. There was no more room to expand, not that the school saw an increase in population. Rather, the 250 students grades K-12 fit nicely in the school. We could not, however, offer any additional extra curricular courses to students beyond the basics required for a Regents diploma of the 1990s. When students sat for exams, it was in the Fire Hall across the street's social hall.I also remember how disheartening it was to see the entire secondary library in a 20 by 20 foot room. Another example of how things were tight included our day. My seventh grade class in the afternoon was interrupted, with the students leaving after 60 minutes to eat lunch and then returning for the last 12 minutes of class. It was nearly impossible to use that time. The loss of 12 minutes a day was brutal. It was an example in my mind of a system trying desperately to make a structure work that was not right, all due to lack of resources and size.

A number of community members expressed severe opposition to merging. Not uncommon (I have written about the phenomenon in other, more scholarly outlets). They did not want to lose the school. They did not want their students sent to a neighboring community. Teacher aides and cafeteria workers were afraid the merger would take away their jobs, the only source of employment in the area. Some teachers were afraid of losing their jobs as well. One of the most poignant memories I have about that fall was seeing some of my students and their parents dressed in school colors, yelling save our school, and save our mascot. They carried signs on the sidewalk near the entrance to the building on Main Street in the heart of the village. Parents asked their students to quit extra curricular activities to protest, and the students did.

This experience which I lived through launched me on a quest to research rural schools and their experiences. This was a deeply influential moment in my life. I saw a community struggling to keep what little was left. Even though the village was the home of the county government, there wasn't much to attract people in the area. A chain sub shop in the gas station provided lunch and dinner to a bachelor who frankly was exhausted from work. Fast food was a 15 minute drive away in the city to the south. Many nights, exhausted, I caved and ordered out. Bad for my waistline.

After the annexation went down in defeat, the school tried to figure out how to carry on. We did. After all, there were two teachers at each grade level until middle school, when there were two teachers per department, except for the single specialist teachers, and part timers through the local cooperative systems, called BOCES. Through the fall I began to understand how connected everyone in the school was to each other. I also realized how connected the community was to its school. In rural America there are some powerful connections between the school and the community. Especially in the Adirondacks, southern tier and the Catskills, the schools and the communities are almost synonymous. Lots of crucial research in my dissertation explores these very points (Jakubowski, 2020).

As the year progressed, we had a number of medical leaves hit our campus. My mentor teacher went out for surgery, and one of the science teachers left as well. We had a teacher leave for maternity. Did I mention there were two new social studies teachers, a new science teacher, and a number of veteran teachers who were most certainly ready to let you know where you stood? While some offered help as lessons failed, and students were acting out, there was a loneliness in teaching that was soul crushing. I was lonely away from peers, friends, and family. Hint: Hire in cohorts, and establish new teacher support groups, please!

I perceived through impostor syndrome due to really high personal standards, that I wasn't really doing too well, and some of the teachers in the school thought I was arrogant. They also did a phenomenal job of not talking with me, but rather running to the principal for everything. Like the time one of the math teachers took her family (which included a 9th grader in my class) on vacation in the middle of the year. When she asked me for his homework, I replied truthfully, that he had nothing to worry about, and that he could read and outline the two chapters that we were looking at.

My rationale was such: When I went to Disney World, I visited the Epcot Center's World Showcase and visited a bunch of Disneyfied cultures. I also saw the great experiments of the resort and learned a lot about a lot. The teacher, my colleague, had the principal call me in and yelled at me. She felt I wasn't doing enough for her son. A fellow teacher, a member of my union, couldn't talk with me as a colleague or a mentor, but had to bring me in for a principal, parent and teacher conference? Talk about eating your young!

I also noticed that the special education services and Title I services were stretched thin. One of the teachers, a Title I reading teacher, stood out as a mentor who helped me just survive that first year. She later became a principal. Her demeanor, her knowledge, and her expertise were so helpful, especially in dealing with students who were at risk because reading was a foreign language to them. Mrs. June reminded me of some of the work I had accomplished at Fredonia, and how to best translate that learning in a way my students would understand. Out of sheer overwhelming circumstances, I had begun to lecture. Remember, I had six classes, blocked at four different grade levels. There were 18 students average in each class, and a study hall assignment. I couldn't deal with all the preps, all the juggling, and the classroom management issues. The kids who for some reason just couldn't learn drove me crazy.

Maybe it was their maturity levels, or maybe it was mine, but those kids just ticked me off. I couldn't rely on help. Any strategy required balancing classroom management with teaching, and making a thousand little decisions each and every day.

One of my biggest issues with journals, books, and magazines about teaching is how they ignore classroom management at the secondary level. Almost all of it is written for elementary classrooms with "only" 20 or 25 kids. And in elementary schools, they stay put and don't move between different teachers every 50 or 72 minutes. I tried all of the techniques, the verbal warnings, the written warnings, the time outs, the phone calls home. Nothing worked. Oh, and by the way, a bunch of them failed the year before and were repeating. The kids who wanted to learn and excel hated the other kids' behaviors. They would often sit with an exasperated look on their face as I had to, for the 10th or 12th time that week deal with a misbehavior. When you are young, and when you are scared of failure, confrontation is not easy. It is especially true when people act passive aggressive to you.

I experienced workplace bullying in the district. I was a victim of someone who thought their viewpoint was more important than mine. To this day Scope mouthwash brings back horrid and wretched meaning for me. Halitosis in the workplace is an ongoing issue. Apparently I had some. So one of the kind denizens of the district, which was home to a fervent anti-bullying environment, and a place of pride in how each person was supported and was meant to be a critical part of the community, had placed a bottle of Scope and a toothbrush in my mailbox at work. No note attached. No attempt at a "hey, just wanted to FYI you". Nothing. Just the humiliation of a bottle of Scope and a toothbrush. These are teacher mailboxes. They are in the office, out for the world to see—no privacy whatsoever.

What can I say for a school that has seen such young/ rookie teacher turnover? It was like I was reading a troupe book about rural schools. I was living in a reality show about some rural schools. I wasn't happy. I didn't like where I was, and I thought I really couldn't do it again. I decided to resign that spring and look for a new job. The connections with the good kids were hardest to break.

I was going to miss a senior who wanted to go to Fredonia. She never made it there. I was going to miss the pregnant senior, who is now in the latter 2020s applying for Assistant Superintendent jobs, despite being at-risk when I taught. Or my basic training graduate, who gave his parents a huge scare when he quit school because one of the other teachers belittled him.

He had left school without returning his textbook, and I needed his economics textbook back! We were "accountable for all the books" so when I saw him at the local sub place, I asked very nicely for him to come back to class, talk about the full time work he had picked up, and give me back the economics textbook. He did come back. He stayed. He graduated. His two elementary teacher parents were very happy. Their thanks to me was misplaced; all I did was ask for the book back so I would avoid getting in trouble.

As a seventh grade team, we decided to hold back almost 10 students out of 40 who were failing their core courses. One boy stuck out in my mind for how completely the school and community had failed him. I am using a pseudonym, out of respect for him. I hope his life is much better. Matt had failed school last year, and repeated seventh grade my year. He came to school with a constant drippy stuff -up nose. He drew pen marks on himself. He wore the same clothes multiple times. He and his friends should never have been in the same class, but when you only have two sections, it's not like the school is too big to separate them. His home life was broken.

There was extreme poverty there. The father had an undiagnosed learning disability. I do not believe that the family had running water. Yes it is true! In New York and other states, a number of rural communities, up to 20 percent of people live without running water! There were vicious rumors circulating around the village about his parents. I believe that Matt was in pain, emotionally and physically. He received special education and remedial services due to his issues. What I really thought was necessary was a do-over, and help from a mental health clinician. This kid was into motorcycles, and dirt racing but he wasn't into school. To think that in 1997-1998 he was a seventh grader, and by 1998-1999, he failed seventh grade again,and had to repeat it in 1999-2000. The only thing I can think of is the opening prayer Catholics use for confession: "Bless me Father, for I have sinned," I committed the act of not helping that young man who needed my help.

Matt—I am forever sorry I could not help you. It weighs heavily on my mind. For all of the students in that first year at my school, I really hope you are successful in your career. Education as a system does not do a good enough job of supporting young teachers as we are practicing. In many careers, there is a ladder of responsibility—an apprenticeship. Teaching tosses you in after one semester of student teaching. We gotta do better. We MUST prevent novice mistakes that lead to educational screw ups.

I feel that there is a bit of irony with my first job, and especially because I love history. One of the books that I loved in undergrad was *The Adventures of Ibn Battuta* by Ross E Dunn. Ross grew up and attended school in the district. It is amazing that there is where I first taught, in the school which graduated Dr. Dunn.

As the school wound down, I faced what many young teachers face. I needed a second job to make ends meet, and I got one as a doughnut fryer. This summer employment was to bridge the gap as I started to take a graduate course in Teaching World History at University at Buffalo. I would come home from frying the doughnuts and setting out the baker's materials and then go to work to supervise finals. I was exhausted. Once the school year ended, I would travel almost 20 miles to do my overnight shift and then return home to sleep. After a while, I quit frying doughnuts. It wasn't safe, and I felt gross all the time. I then moved back with mom and dad and took a job as a fundraiser for an environmental group. Our job, based out of really crappy offices in downtown Buffalo, was to go door-to-door and say a pre-written speech, asking people to sign a petition and donate money. We kept half of the funds we raised each night. We needed to get at least 200 dollars a night to keep our employment.

Since I am not a salesperson, I lasted three weeks, and then was "not renewed" for the next week. By this time, I was also interviewing for jobs again. I realized that there is a tight network among school admins. They also protect each other. Once I ran into a good friend of my former principal. When he asked me why I resigned, I told him I didn't feel supported. He informed me the interview was over but he was going to give me some coaching. He coached me that the answer I gave wasn't a very good one, and I should say, "Oh for personal reasons." That was the best advice I ever received. I would be moving to Central New York to follow a love interest. I did not realize that this move would start the darkest period of my life, and hurt me and my family to no end.

REFLECTIONS:

- What are the triumphs from your first year of teaching?
- How have you improved over your teaching career?
- In what ways would you mentor a new teacher in your opinion?

[8]

THE EARLY TEACHING YEARS

The more things change, the more the saying goes! Out of element, and adding to my life as a newly minted adult, I was in for this experience.

Guiding question: Have you wondered what if? Create a career map of what will, or what did happen. How will these events impact you?

BACKGROUND

After leaving my first teaching job, we moved halfway across the state to a very rural county. It is so rural that it is in the bottom 15 out of 66. Its major city, Norwich, was the home to Norwich Aspirin. The county was bisected by the Chenango Canal, which linked the Erie Canal to the Susquehanna River, and the big cities of Philly and Baltimore. The county is covered in rolling hills and dairy farms. It is spotted with large state forests and the ruins of farmsteads which have collapsed as the dairy industry deteriorated. The county is dotted with little villages, all about 8-10 miles apart, having in past days been the market communities for their rural agricultural operations. The nearest large cities are Binghamton to the south, a forty mile drive, and Utica to the north, almost 40 miles as well. To the east lies Oneonta, and its two colleges: Hartwick and SUNY Oneonta. The west has Cortland, and Ithaca beyond that. On our first night in a large three bedroom apartment, my partner and I ate chain pizza, and shopped at a local store of a Western New York based grocery chain (no not the W one!). The little city had just enough to make life okay, such as a bookstore and a big box retailer. It was a walkable city for sure. We lived close to the middle and high school, and had a wide lawn in our apartment complex. As I was applying for jobs in the area, it became clear that I was most likely going to have to substitute. But then, almost on the first of September, I applied for and was hired into a district that was close, a small district of about 1000 students fifteen minutes away in Delaware county. Delaware county is even smaller, and is the 10th smallest county in New York, with 47,000 people. My new teaching home is one of the two largest schools in the county, with another one in the heart of Delaware County as the other. My interview with the superintendent revealed we are both Eagle Scouts. It was nice to see how our connection would help me have a shot at work I cared about. Service to community and education are often careers, and leadership from scouting can have a positive, life long impact. Being a leader means advocating for others. The term is sponsorship. As a person with power, or position, you need to see people who will do well, and provide a nudge for them in the right direction.

My job at the school this first year was to serve as a building substitute for the high school. It was my duty to fill in for teachers who were out, and more importantly help serve as back up with the special education staff in the building.The community is centered around and in a village which is home to a major manufacturing plant for air and space parts. The village used to host a hospital, so there was some level of professional class in the community. The village was home to two grocery stores, a Great American and a Grand Union. The village sits at the confluences of two major watersheds in central New York. Before the American Revolution, the area to the west of these rivers was off limits to British settlers when the Proclamation Line of 1763 was put into effect by the British crown. The village contains a small airfield which hosts a fly- in pancake breakfast once a year. But what hits you the most about this area are the deep valleys that have eroded or glaciated themselves in the ice age. Their undulation divides communities up into isolated villages along rivers. The roads cut ribbons across and above the hills.

I started my work in central New York as a permanent substitute— my job entailed serving for teachers who were out that day. The job began as a way to initially fill a gap in the number of available substitutes, and provide students with some stability in the classroom. In this role, I became quite attached to the special education department as I provided an extra body in the resource room. I also found myself tutoring after school frequently, as it was a way to earn extra cash.

This kismet, or opportunity of happenstance, during my first year introduced me to a reading and writing specialist who taught at night at Binghamton university. Lynn is one of those people who you wish there were more of in the world. It was a crazy whirlwind of activity that first year. I never knew where I would be from one day to the next. I was lent out on occasion to the middle school and to the elementary school to help fill in for other teachers who were out. My favorite class to work with in middle school was the seventh grade. Since I had taught seventh grade, I was familiar with the curriculum and the pedagogy. In high school , I enjoyed the social studies department, of course. What was amazing to me that first year was the gap between the professional's children in the village and the rural kids. In fact, data from the school indicated student achievement levels from the two outlying elementary schools did not do well when transitioning to the middle school.

I also undertook my first action research project this first year. A couple of seniors had yet to pass the Global History and Geography exam needed to graduate. When they failed the tests (for some of them , it was their 8th attempt), I did a data analysis of their past exams. By hand, I went back and looked at the number of errors in the multiple choice. I figured out which areas geographically they were missing, and developed a set of flashcards for tutoring. The flash cards had the words and a symbol on the front and the definition and one question on the back (multiple choice). So I worked with those seniors as much as I could until they knew that Gandhi from India resisted imperialism, and humanism of the Renaissance meant that all people were good. We discussed how documents on the test in the essay section could help write the Document Based Essay Question, and that you needed one piece of outside info to score a three out of five. We worked on these efforts until the students raised their grades from 49 and 52 points to 55 and 65 points. They passed. They graduated. They got to go on with their lives as nurses, mechanics, soldiers. And I found myself hooked on research. I wanted to write and tell the world about this technique. I liked working with students who struggled. I saw a little bit of my brother in them. He tried hard to understand, but the teachers just didn't know how to translate it into a different way for him.

Over that first summer, I was invited to serve as a faculty member for a summer remedial program designed to help at-risk 8th grade students learn some skills to prepare them for high school. The students, 12 in all, were struggling with school—reading and writing, research, math and science. They had poor organization skills, and needed prompting to remember academic tasks. Almost all 12 received special education services. We decided as a faculty to be creative in our approach to pedagogy with this group. Our aim was clear: teach them survival skills which are needed to find success in high school.

Summer schools are often taught just like the regular school year—repetitive and lecture heavy. There is quite often little innovation involved as the students are subjected to a regurgitation which summarizes the materials from the regular year. We decided to preview the coming attractions. We wanted to help our students get ready for high school. First step in the process was team teaching. Our goal was to work in pairs, with the ELA teacher and me as social studies teacher offering a humanities block every other day. The science and math teachers would tag-team in their block every other day. We integrated the content and the skills by merging the texts that students would read. Our approach was heavy into experiential learning.

We took the students to a chain book store in Binghamton where they selected a book they wanted to read. Yes, you read correctly. The students could choose whatever book they wanted to read. Period, no question mark, no oversight except for some gentle nudging. A grant from the local Parent Teacher Association covered the cost of the book. That independent read became a focal point for the students learning about technology or a person. For our students, they leaned towards science, fiction, and action books. It was really nice to see the students engaged in looking for and at books, and reading them. When we returned to the community, the students had ownership of the books, and were more than willing to share what they learned.

Our big project that summer was investigating the local Pioneer Cemetery. It is located right next to the community library. The burials on site are old, going back to the late 1700s and early 1800s. The students were asked to find out about the grave markers and investigate the people who were buried there. Our students created reports about who they found, what they discovered about the person, and what some of the international events the individual may have been around to see or hear about.

In a moment that will enliven any teacher's heart, one of the students found out that a soldier from the War of 1812 was buried in the cemetery, and that set us off on a chase through the national archives and records administration, and the local county Historical society. That event really brought home the historical research aspect that was missing from many students' experiences in social studies. It also encouraged me to think about how we use classroom and local resources to expand our students' learnings. Later that summer, I was interviewed for a position with the district that would be 60% social studies and 40% working with at-risk students in a high school equivalency prep program. I found I enjoyed the job—at work by 10:00am, teaching three sections of Global 10, and working until 6:30pm at night with students who needed help. It was a very nice set-up. It allowed me to work with students who had not gotten along with the school system as it was traditionally set up. I was also invited to attend a field trip along with superintendents and principals to an alternative school in a different BOCES. This was my first real exposure to seeing administration as a potential career path.

My next year teaching social studies at the district was a change. By year three, I was asked to take over a College in the High School program. This class was a college level class which some seniors took instead of the Participation in Government class in order to graduate. That summer, I was sent to the regional university and trained over the course of a week in how to teach the course. I was simultaneously appointed as an adjunct instructor at the University! My course load included three Global 10 classes at and one Participation in Government and one college in the high school class. I was also asked to lead a club that year, so I founded a Future Teachers of America in the district. We sent students into the elementary school to help out for one day a month. Many came home and were exhausted.

The college in the high school program students were expected to travel up to the University Library to research their papers and tour the campus once a semester. I thought it would be great to arrange this trip for my future teachers as well, and we did the next year—so that we could expose the students to college on the big time level.

My second year I started grad school in a regional university Master of History program. In order to make money to keep the body, soul and roof over my head, I needed to work in the summer too. The summer of my second and third year, I taught Summer School at the BOCES to help earn extra money. I was teaching 9th grade summer school. It was a very intense 3 hours. Our schedule was arranged so that we saw two sections of students. It was very hot in our rooms—at a local regional southern site one year and a northern site the next. None of the schools had air conditioning, and the sun beat down on the eastern side of the buildings creating a hot room with no air movement. Now, in COVID -19 era, we are finally seeing debate on the need for high quality air and temperature control. It is a national shame our nation treats our children so poorly in such poor conditions.

That year I was diagnosed as a type II diabetic. I have struggled with this fact for my entire life. It is painful and horrid. Food is your enemy. Your appetite is an attack upon your very being. Sleep does not come and when it does, it is interrupted. I also was tested for sleep apnea. Between the diabetes and potential apnea (which is now diagnosed) my body wouldn't allow me to function. I was also having issues at home. My marriage was breaking up and it was affecting my daily life. That fourth year, among two classes for grad school, my involvement with scouts, and my marriage falling apart, I hit bottom, or so I thought.

I needed an escape, so I dove into, as much as possible, a passion-sharing information with others! I found that I liked research, and was presenting at the New York State Social Studies conference, and writing articles in the *Social Science Docket* (now *Teaching Social Studies*). However, I found that I was hating graduate school. I was finding my writing wasn't good, according to my instructors. This is a problem all over academia, because the profession is all about critique and not scaffold and support. As a society, we must face a huge issue: many graduate schools are full of very hurtful people, who intentionally or not intentionally, are more concerned with abstract concepts like prestige, rather than educating and creating a well engaged person.

I went that summer between my fourth and fifth year to a full week of social studies professional development sponsored by a Teaching American History Grant. We learned to look at documents to create lessons around the Civil Rights Movement. I also began to notice I was drifting away from my fellow teachers. I was seeing patterns and events and streams in history they were missing, but I could not make sense in Grad classes about these issues. I was beginning to feel like I did not belong in a high school classroom. I also felt like I did not really belong with the researchers. I felt like I had a foot in both worlds, but wasn't really a part of either. This feeling has settled in me, and nagged at the back of my mind. Too "brainy" in some ways, an "intellectual lightweight" in others.

My marriage broke up, and I broke down. During my fifth year, I decided to go home to Buffalo. I resigned with an expected date at the end of June. That year, the principal decided he wanted to become a superintendent, so he made life miserable for all the untenured teachers. He took a department that had three future PhDs and real historians and made it into a shadow of itself. As a system, schools are overly concerned with gaining peak performance out of teachers. However, the systems do not provide the scaffolding that is needed. The system is designed to toss anyone not conforming out.

How I wished I would have had help as I was journeying in the dark, twisted and exhausted state of my days. Mental health professionals did not help. Medication did not help. I struggled with depression. And the year would become worse. This was also the year we lost one of our graduates in Iraq. He was killed by an IED. As our school was in mourning for our lost soldier, one of our student's dad was killed in an auto accident. This was followed up by a suicide by a student. How can we be strong for our students when we are weak and weeping ourselves? I remember the day that the churches, each and everyone in the village opened for our students, our faculty, our staff and residents. That was the week from hell. I was to find out much later one of the teachers I knew and respected and loved also passed due to suicide. The school community has lost too many people. The system of education is more concerned about ideas and metrics, and performance than people. Don't misunderstand me. Not all schools are like this, but if you scratch the surface, in many places, the systems are brutal survival of the fittest. It is almost like the adults never emotionally left the tables in the cafeteria. For all the anti-bullying initiatives that are reported out of education, and for all the legislation from states and the federal government, scratch the surface of many schools, and find a swirling war zone of horrible angry people. Maybe this phenomenon comes from ambition, or from lack of appreciation. I know that a ton of educators are doing the right thing, and are striving at the risk of their own health. Yet there are just some horrid rots in the system. And I became a statistic. I was one of the 50% of teachers who leave within five years (Dias-Lacy & Guirguis, 2017). Broken and in massive pain, I wanted to go home. And so I went home. My family packed me up and we left the day of graduation and I headed back home.

REFLECTIONS:

- How does your personal life as a teacher impact your professional life?
- What are some skills/ techniques for reducing the severity of this impact?

[9]
STARTING OVER

What does it mean to start over? Is it persistence, grit, growth mindset, or disparity? As a field we celebrate triumphs but never really address our failures and defeats. This chapter re-focuses my career into the "adjacent" fields of education.

Guiding question: What skills/ abilities do you possess that are not "teacher" based? What else would you do?

At home, I spent the summer volunteering at a day camp for the scouts. I connected with old friends and made new ones. The mental and emotional support also allowed me to finish my Master's degree and write my final paper. I graduated in August with a Master's degree. My capstone paper was a look into state records concerning the history of the many consolidation attempts by a small rural district. I researched the archive and found a treasure trove of stories that are in a box waiting for rediscovery. I found I wanted to tell the consolidation story to a wider audience. Rural America gets short shrift in the research world (Jakubowski, 2020). A number of authors talk about rural US as a deficiency (Azano & Biddle, 2018). I tell you it is a story about survival and overcoming the odds. New York State has so many rural areas, and yet we don't hear about the amazing activities that the people have, host and do daily.

That fall, I was a paid program site lead for the local scout council working with inner city urban schools running a leadership and character development program. We spent September-December working with students on communication, team building exercises, and responsibilities. This effort was rewarding, but difficult, as many of the public schools were struggling with classroom discipline, and quite often the students were not allowed to work with us in our experiential activities. This was my first real exposure to the Charter School movement. The charter school movement is a private attempt to horn in on the public money stream in education. For many early charter school reformers, they had a very noble goal: provide children a better educational opportunity than they were receiving in the public schools which geography had required them to attend. Charter school advocates believe that a zip code should not decide a child's fate. The reform movement also stated the same thing, as did Johnson's War on Poverty. We need to reconceptualize schools in distressed areas as social service providers, not just educational endeavors. Jeff Canada and Harlem Children's Zone attempted to provide students with education, medical, social and emotional support services. While at the City Public Schools and the Charter schools, I noticed a strong emphasis on discipline and a subtle resignation by the faculty. The charter school teachers frequently turned over. No tenure contracts there. They were highly paid compared to some of their public school colleagues. One social studies teacher at the charter school was from another state. He had no idea what he was preparing the students for on the end of year exams. A science teacher looked like he was going to have a stroke at any moment. The special education teacher was an emergency hire.

The school was run by two administrators from overseas. One would later attend classes with me to earn his administrator certificate. The middle-high school was held in an old church and school building designed for elementary grade students.

Many of the students who wanted to learn science were forced to use paper labs, just like in the underfunded public schools in the large city. The physical size of the kids and the physical size of the building did not work too well. I loved hearing from one of the teachers at the school, the church in which they were renting space thought the kids were too loud, and needed to be quiet. The only time the students had any social time was in the hallways or the cafeteria. The food provided by the public school was less than appetizing. Heavy on carbs and sugars, it was steamed when it arrived from a central "kitchen." A diet such as what we feed our kids in school is driving malnutrition—not from lack of carbs, but lack of understanding what a healthy meal looks like. The food should not have been a microwave dinner quality.

The students spent a lot of time in classrooms. Extra hours after school. Extra time in the summer. This philosophy harkened back to a chance meeting, with a retired air force officer teaching social studies at another school in the rural New York area. He said at a conference and I wrote this down, because I was shocked: "pound 'em with facts till their ears bleed." What a great way to inspire learning. At this urban based charter school, and others that I have interacted with over the years, there is a strong emphasis on rote memorization. The work in the charter school and my own dissonance with the philosophy I saw egged me on to apply to adjunct. After all, with a Master's degree and living with my parents, why not.

In December, I was invited to a local comprehensive college to interview for an adjunct position in the History Department. During this time I would teach classes on world and US history at odd hours. I also started taking classes at University at Buffalo in the area of Teacher Mentoring. I wanted to know what had gone wrong in my own journey and how to fix it. I enjoyed teaching college, and was lucky that I was able to teach two classes over the summer. That fall, I added teaching at Niagara University and Niagara County Community College to my portfolio.

As I was teaching at the colleges, I found myself engaged in amazing conversations with my fellow department members. I enjoyed learning about the tenure system. I became very close to Jean Richardson, an expert in Buffalo History. I had some great conversations with the faculty there about the teaching and learning of both History and Social Studies. I enjoyed working with the students as I asked them to tease out the story behind the history of the world, the US and later, briefly New York. I enjoyed teaching classes where the students gave the impression of wanting to be in school. Many students were majoring in the field I was teaching. Quite a few took the class as an elective. All of them thought my humor corny at best, terrible at worst.

During the time I was at the three schools I realized that the higher ed system in the US has some really varied levels of expectation. At the community college, the demands of the professors were almost more strict than many four year schools. At the private liberal arts college the teachers who taught 20th century US history all had to prepare for a department final that our entire classes took. At the comprehensive state college, we were much more free to teach our course the way we wished to. My experience happened before the accreditation craze happened, and we needed to collect evidence of everything.

I am amazed how our system in the US works. As a student in elementary and secondary education, you are tested on standardized tests because politicians do not trust your teachers and demand accountability (Ravitch & Stoher, 2017). When you are in college, you not only get a grade from a professor, but to enter some professions, you need to take and pass licensure exams. The authority to educate is delegated to colleges and universities and teachers, all of whom have advanced degrees, yet none of which is trusted by a legislature who are not often educators. This lack of trust is rampant throughout American society. Parents don't trust kids—they have a GPS tracking device on cell phones. We have nanny cams and home monitoring systems. Somehow, having a professional's training and an education is no longer enough. At work, spyware will tell our employers what sites on the internet we visit, and record our emails. The deprofessionalization of the professional classes harkens back to the paternalism that industrial barons used towards unskilled labor, and imperialists used to justify colonialism.

I also saw the adjunctification of higher education in action. I needed to teach those five classes at three institutions almost 40 miles in travel apart to make $35,000 in 2004. I had to live at home to afford to pay bills. The system's current reliance on adjuncts has created a situation where best practices of education have been sacrificed to some other goal—be it "efficiency" or "compliance" or in many ways as a result of the systematic defunding of education in the US. While the sheer volume of resources has increased, the actual real impact has steeply declined. What is worse, industry has thrown all of the demands for training onto schools and universities, deemed the job poorly done, and retrained graduates their way and continue to complain in platforms that the education system is a wreck and failing. Big businesses do this while not paying a red cent in taxes, and shifting burdens to other taxpayers to underwrite their costs for training.

One of the joys I discovered teaching was the access to the libraries to actually conduct research. I had put aside rural schools for the moment and began to focus on mentoring teachers and recording my social studies teaching experience. I look back with pride on the presentations I gave at the New York State Council for the Social Studies conferences. I also loved the fact that some brief articles found their way into the *Social Science Docket* (now *Teaching Social Studies*), a state level publication for the New York and the New Jersey Councils for Social Studies.

While taking classes in teacher mentoring, I found out how important mentoring new teachers is to the professional and personal careers in education. Almost fifty percent of teachers who enter the profession leave within the first five years. Half. That is approximately the same percentage of NFL players who are cut every year after training camp. (An NFL preseason roster is 90 players. 53 players are kept on the roster for the regular season). Teachers leave the profession for a number of reasons: lack of pay, poor working conditions, alienation, family responsibilities, enormous professional pressure. The worst offensive process must be an evaluation system which states that a principal can tell a teacher in their first four years that they are not good enough for any reason and reject them.

And since the educational world is so small, many teachers who are forced to resign, or denied tenure, or are laid off due to the constant underfunding of public education, find it difficult to find a job in a career which so many bright people who really want to work with students, who really want to help at risk and challenged children make it, are tossed out like yesterday's guacamole. Mentors are needed to help novice teachers navigate the first year in the profession. In fact, New York State now requires that all first year teachers be mentored. Unfortunately a number of studies indicate that the fifth year of teaching is the pivot point, where novices begin to really demonstrate competency as practitioners.

For me personally, my mentoring was short, abbreviated, and did not address the largest problem that forces teachers out of small districts: They are not from the area. A number of studies indicate that teachers prefer to be close to home when they land a teaching position (Miller, 2012) . In fact, they want to be within fifty miles of home, and work at a similar school to what they grew up in. In the two rural districts I worked in, I saw the "outsiders" to the local community leave. Some left voluntarily to find positions closer to home, or in a suburban district. Others were forced to leave because they did not fit the "culture." To me, the "I'm sorry, you don't fit the culture" line is bull. It's an excuse because the teacher was rocking the boat by raising standards, or asking children to read something that the local community didn't like. The outsider may have been sacrificed so that an administrator could clear the way for a child of a teacher to join the family profession. The administrator's personal ambition may have required the sacrifice. Advancement in the education profession is interesting, as so many nice people become horrible managers.

All that aside, a good mentor will help teachers deal with parents who may question the capabilities of a young, early career educator, and cannot possibly know how to deal with their child. A strong mentor can help the new teacher learn how to write lesson plans that the administration will not red flag. Mentors can work with the new teacher to navigate the 100s of hours of administrative crap that comes their way. This includes filling out forms for all manner of requisitions, and data sheets for specialists, and keeping a grade book, which is a legal document. The mentor can protect the young teacher from the cabals which lurk in the lounge, or the bullies who masquerade as colleagues. A mentor can guide new teachers as they attempt to balance their professional demands of a job, a required graduate degree, and maybe committee involvement or club advising or coaching.

A mentor is an advisor to help improve your in classroom craft. The mentor can discuss a lesson, from the inception stage to the evaluation and plan for next year's stage. They can help teachers look at the overwhelming level of data that is collected each year on behavior, tests, quizzes, homework, exit tickets, entry tickets and projects. When the avalanche of everything strikes at once, a good mentor can help a teacher wade through and triage every single important thing that needs to be done with the urgency of critical care.

Professional educators are driven, and haunted, by the realization that each child gets one chance with a life. Research studies have shown two important points: If a teacher believes in a student, the student can find success, and two bad teachers in a row doom kids to almost dropping out of school. While working with the students who had failed the Global exam, and needed to pass the test to graduate, I discovered that many were classified as learning disabled. More shocking and upsetting, as I was reviewing my notes in preparation for an article, I had scribbled a note on Annie's papers (name made up to protect the innocent and not so innocent): They gave up.

It wasn't the students. It was some of the teachers. None of the teachers actively gave up on the kids. They just stopped refusing to allow the kids to fail. This is a sign of burnout, and the education profession is seriously susceptible to the damage done when a teacher has become so overwhelmed by the massive uphill battle faced every year. Standards become raised, initiatives created, the students need more support. It becomes overwhelming.

Larry Maheady and Barb Mallette at Fredonia instilled in us a deep and sacred obligation to never give up. These two amazing professors were special education faculty at SUNY Fredonia who taught the Introduction to Exceptional Education class required of all teaching majors. Larry (please forgive my informality) in one class went through a routine about compliance, defiance, and how we could overcome this. If a student says "I forgot my pencil," you provide a pencil. If they forgot their book, have a spare. If they forgot the homework, give a second copy.

As I was reflecting on my life and career in the middle of the mentoring teachers courses, I re-read some of my college papers. I realized that I learned so much at Fredonia and I could not put it all in play because I was juggling the massive number of stressors of a job, medical illness, and a failing marriage. I wish I had taken more time with my mentor to discuss the guided homework sheets I tried to implement. The idea was to give students a way to plan their week. Every Friday, they would get a photocopy from me of homework, topics covered in class, and five new vocabulary words for the unit.

My mentor would have given me some feedback, and helped me make the guided homework easier to implement. Larry and Barb would have been thrilled I was scaffolding my class to support at risk learners. Mind you this strategy happened before the internet, phones, text messages, and the learning platforms now part of the profession.

Larry and Barb would have been thrilled to note that I was implementing Team Based Competition. The idea here is to have students create a visual flash card with the vocabulary word on the front of the 3x5 index card and a drawing that represents the concept. On the back of the card, the definition of the term would appear. Also on the back, the student would put the context for the word with an illustrative example. In class, the goal was for student pairs to get through as many vocabulary words in 2 minutes as possible. They would switch partners. Their decks would start out at 20 and increase by 5 each unit. After the student got a card right for 5 straight rounds, the card was retired. My mentor would have helped me make this more effective. The national research is there. It works with students. I was having trouble with the classroom management mechanics to make it work.

As I reflected on my teaching career with the mentoring classes, it became abundantly clear that I had failed as a secondary educator. I fit the old adage of those who can't do, teach. Feeling like a failure is not what someone does when they have a support network and an Eagle award. I started the course work in the teacher mentoring program at UB to make a difference, and to make sure no one suffered as badly as I did. I also began to take classes which interested me in administration. I enrolled in a class called "Action Research" with Bob Stevenson. An Australian who had a wit as sharp as a tack, Bob was devoted to the idea of action research. He taught us how to study what we did in the classroom as objectively as possible using all manner of data collection techniques. I can say with profound truth I gained so much insight about my teaching style from that class. I also enjoyed meeting some of the administrators from the area working on their PhDs.

The second class I learned a lot from examined different perspectives on staff development. I really enjoyed examining how staff development worked, or failed to work, and began to notice patterns in how unsuccessful my own personal experience in staff development left me wanting a greater experience. From the school based staff development I learned that many of the programs are geared towards elementary school teachers and elementary ideas. There are very few rigorous programs in staff development which really address the needs of secondary teachers. From the Binghamton University Teaching American History program, insight emerged which allowed me to understand how intellectually rigorous some schools were in the area, but many schools were struggling due to lack of resources to just survive.

During my time learning about Teacher Mentoring, I learned not enough schools pay real attention to the need for outstanding professional development. If we really want to make a difference in the lives of teachers and students, we need a profession that is encouraged to take professional time to learn. Too many politicians are calling for more "efficiency" in education, with more teachers working with more students. This model is incorrect and dangerous to our nation. Simon Sinek once said "Get to your why!" Education has failed to tell the why really. We spend so much time on the what and the how that we as a profession have allowed others to claim our why and spread it for their agenda.

REFLECTIONS:

- As professionals, we know people who need to change places. How have you helped or hindered a peer who needed your help in moving along?
- What techniques do you favor for helping students?

[10]

#IMPOSTORSYNDROME

How do you deal with impostor syndrome? This chapter explores those thoughts, as I struggled to find my way past impostor syndrome and find my way as a professional. The events are scary. We change and we feel like we do not belong. How do we overcome this fear?

Guiding question: What do you do to overcome your feeling of impostor? What works well and what has not?

The sun coming up over the Atlantic Ocean is a sight to see. The vision of the magnificent aqua blue is calming. You get a sense of awe as the sun's rays touch the ocean waves , with a salt tinged breeze driving the gulls into looping dives and glides. The eastern part of Long Island is dotted with old estates and farms, harkening back to the fishing village days and whaling ports that made the east end of the island a refuge from the Atlantic storms. The north fork of the island is agriculture in nature, and has vineyards and roadside stands. The homey feeling of the pine barrens slowly gives away to the south fork's tourist Hamptons, with the large mansions, crowded beaches, and traffic as long as one cannot stand. Working your way back west, towards the city, you run into smaller, poorer communities, which are home to the workers who make Long Island's economy hum. Along the south shore immigrant communities struggle to integrate into the white working class areas founded after World War II.

Levittown, one of the most famous prefab housing circles, sits now as its own community in Nassau County. Along the Long Island Railroad stops, many of these communities became the bedrooms for New York City workers seeking to flee beyond the outer boroughs and into suburbia. Long Island is a very segregated part of New York State (Rothstein, 2015). Just like many of the urban areas, a few specific communities in Long Island are heavily minority. The data and the school community demographics are shocking from one town to the next. Hempstead, NY is almost completely a minority- majority school district. Wyandanch schools, surrounded on all sides, are almost 100 % minority as a school system. Roosevelt, the only school district completely taken over by New York State, has almost no white children attending its schools (NYSED Data 2012).

These school districts are comparatively poorer than their more affluent neighbors. They house some of the poorest children in Long Island, well within sight of the wealthiest communities in the county. Not only are the schools poor, but they have a difficult time meeting state test standards. New York State's Education department received so many complaints and poor media coverage of the Roosevelt, Wyandanch, and Hempstead Union Free School Districts on Long Island, the Commissioner tasked an entire department to deal with the crisis of Long Island's poorest communities (NYSED press releases). By every stretch of the imagination, the " Long Island three" has suffered from a wide variety of problems. Within their community, poverty, violence, and substance abuse created a horrible situation. In the 1980s, the New York State Education Department created a system of school reviews designed to call out the poor standards of education in schools across the state. Unsurprisingly, New York City, and the "Big 4" cities of Buffalo, Rochester, Syracuse and Yonkers had schools which appeared on the "school under registration review" list. Essentially, this list told the school district, and by extension, the public, that the school itself was in such poor condition academically that the state was mandating change. If change was not implemented and successful, the school could be terminated, or registration revoked, and could not be trusted to issue graduation certificates or implement the K-8 standards which would allow students to move on to high school. What came as a bit of a surprise was the Roosevelt, Wyandanch, and Hempstead schools all wound up on the School Under Registration Review (SURR) list.

After a series of *Newsday* articles, and some *New York Times* articles, the state education department and the legislature began to hear even more issues and problems out of the three school districts. Finally, the Board of Regents, in conjunction with the legislature, passed a law which stripped Roosevelt of the right to elect its own Board of Education members. They were to be appointed by the Commissioner of Education and that office would appoint a superintendent. This followed significant financial irregularities on top of the academic issues which faced the district. The State Education Department appointed a whole team of employees, including an Assistant Commissioner, to monitor the school district and meet with its leadership on a regular basis. At the monthly Board of Regents meetings, status updates on the district were presented to the Regents. The district was taken over by the state. The action of taking over a district is an unprecedented step in a state which prides itself on local control of education.

While teaching at Buffalo State College, Niagara University, and working on an advanced degree at University at Buffalo, I saw a posting for a school improvement job for the state. It asked for 5 years of teaching experience and a master's degree. I was floored that I qualified. So I applied, and was invited for an interview in Albany. I drove out, stayed overnight with friends of the family, and interviewed to work as a school improvement liaison for the state. The job was to review and approve school improvement funds and plans based upon the No Child Left Behind federal regulations. I would be asked to travel to Long Island and review the progress on site that the schools were making with the school improvement plans, called Restructuring plans. The districts in restructuring had, by 2006, been part of the progressive federal plan to make penalties harsher for schools which failed the yearly testing requirements. A Restructuring school in 2006 was in the cycle for every year that the penalties had existed.

An even deeper level of accountability were the New York State Schools under Registration Review (SURR). This initiative, launched by the state in the 1990s, resulted from a series of media reports about how ineffective some schools were in the inner city. The idea behind the SURR schools reform involved the District being asked to do more for the schools by focusing additional resources into the buildings in trouble. In a larger area like New York City, this may have been a good strategy, but for school districts like Roosevelt, Wyandanch, and Hempstead, the districts were smaller and did not have the infrastructure to really make an improvement in the high schools.

As I announced my departure, many of my colleagues were excited for me. I left the adjunct track and now moved into a government position. Some of my colleagues conveyed hope I could actually make a difference in schools. One colleague had told me, and I'm paraphrasing a bit, to "tell the superintendents how to get it right!" This quote brings out an interesting bit of cognitive dissonance in perception and reality that citizens maintain concerning government ability and oversight power.

There is a perception among many citizens that state government is powerful, and can actually intervene in school and district problems. After all, the state has the responsibility for oversight and enforcement right? My reality and experience provided a major "insider look" into what actual and real powers state governments can exercise. Governors and state political leaders often talk about the change they want to make. Officials talk about the neoliberal goal of equity for all through government action. Many officials feel that they are demonstrating leadership by publicly commenting on an issue. New York, and elsewhere, often give in theory great powers to superintendents, principals, boards of education, and others to do something. We are a state impacted by the need for speed, and action. New York City, Seneca Falls, and other areas throughout the state have witnessed protests against injustice, and the slow speed of change. Yet in education, and state government, speed does not always translate to action.

My first day of work at SED was a whirlwind of a building tour and meeting people across offices and responsibilities. The State Education Department is housed in multiple buildings across New York State. The SED many people think about is the beautiful classic building on Washington Avenue in Downtown Albany. It is augmented by a hideous 1960s cube annex called the EBA. Originally built in the early 1900s as the offices and museum of the State Education Department, the rapid increase in bureaucratization throughout the mid 20th century resulted in the museum moving across the Rockefeller Plaza into a new building designated as the Cultural Education Center that contained the museum, archives and the state library. You could see in the Ed Building the glorious past as a museum, archives, and library. The main hall of the building, nicknamed Commissioner's Hall, has paintings of each Commissioner of Education back to the founding President of the University of the State of New York and Commissioner of Education. New York is unique as it is placed under the control of a Board of Regents every single educational function of the state. Starting out as the Board of Regents of Kings (later Columbia University) College in the 1700s, the oversight organization evolved to supervise not only higher education, but elementary education, museums, archives, libraries, historical societies, and professional certification for a wide number of professions, from cosmetology to medical doctor. State Ed started small (Folts, 1996) with a Commissioner and a secretary to the Board of Regents, but grew as more money was added to the mix.

The Commissioner is selected, supervised, and dismissed by the Board of Regents, who represent each of 13 New York's Judicial districts and 4 at large members. The Board is not elected by popular vote. They are selected by the New York State Legislature, which is composed of an assembly and senate. Due to numbers, the Assembly usually dominates the selection of Regents. Often, these individuals are political leaders in their communities, and some have been educators at the college or university level. Every once in a while, a teacher or principal will be selected to serve as a member. Almost all have advanced education. They are very powerful, and quite often politically connected. Some have been extremely wealthy.

My time in State service countered the often repeated, yet very incorrect perception that state bureaucrats were lazy. I met some of the most amazing people within a department dedicated to helping children experience high quality education. Many believed in their mission. They took the mission of the Department to heart:

Our mission is to raise the knowledge, skill, and opportunity of all the people in New York. Our vision is to provide leadership for a system that yields the best educated people in the world.

Our team was tasked to do the difficult task: ensure all students, especially those in the most vulnerable schools and situations, had an opportunity to receive a world class education. Our team leaders were inspirational. The three truly believed that the work underway was crucial to making a true difference in children's lives. The team was divided into upstate and Long Island. We didn't deal with NYC; that was a different branch out of NYC. This small (only 9 of us to serve all of the state outside of NYC), but dedicated team had the responsibility to monitor the federal Title I grants for school districts in accountability status. Each year, districts submit to the State

Education Department a Consolidated Application for federal Title education funds. The monies were authorized from the original Elementary and Secondary Education Act of 1973, designed to compensate for educational gaps due to poverty- hence its original parlance of "compensatory education." The different funds had very specific guidelines. Title IA is the funding system designed to help students deemed at risk for school issues based on poverty. It is often the largest pot of federal money a school district receives, and is based on the count of children in poverty within the school district's boundaries. Title ID is a fund which is given to schools for institutes for students who are described as neglected or delinquent. Title IIA is given for two purposes: professional development and class size reduction. Title III monies are used to support bilingual and immigrant educational funds. Title IV monies are used for safe schools, while Title V was available for innovative programs. Title VI or REAP is monies specifically designated to help rural schools. Our office reviewed the plans and expenditures for the Titled Monies for the districts we were assigned. For a former high school teacher, used to getting $250 dollars in a classroom budget, looking at a 5 million dollar application was overwhelming!

There were strict guidelines from the federal USDOE on what the monies needed to be used for. For Title IA monies, the districts had to supply schools extra resources by poverty rate. So for instance, a district may fund a reading or math teacher in its elementary school to help children learn how to read. Other schools could fund after-school programs for students to receive tutoring. Many schools chose to fund their high poverty schools with reading or math teachers to help children. We were always checking to ensure schools were following federal regulations and were not supplanting local funds. Supplemental, not supplanting, was one of the key features of federal funding. Essentially, the federal government demanded that schools go beyond what was required by the state for a sound basic education program in order to help students at risk via poverty. If a school was trying to use federal monies to take the place of local taxpayer contributions for core instruction that was supplanting. We needed as a team to guard against school districts artificially keeping local tax rates down by using federal money.

Our other responsibility was to ensure that the districts gave their poorest schools the resources they needed. For many districts, the poorest school did not get the money it needed because schools wanted to help support favored buildings with funds. We were supposed to see which buildings had the highest poverty rates, and the districts needed to contribute the most funds to those schools based on the number of kids in poverty. The schools also had to identify if they would target only the kids in poverty or the whole school (targeted assistance or school wide). Students can be sitting next to each other at lunch and in a classroom and one will get extra help and the other will not—all because of federal requirements. Some school districts would fight decisions to have a school identified as Title I. Those district leaders felt that the federal money wasn't worth the strings attached. Or the districts wouldn't designate a school as a Title I school to ensure that other, less poor schools got the money. It's all legal according to regulations.

When a school did enter accountability under No Child Left Behind, there were penalties that were assessed against a school and district. We were the team which ensured the district recognized those penalties and enacted the penalties. There were a series of penalties I will lay out for you. Step one: First, if the school district did not have 100% highly qualified teachers, the federal government made the districts take 5% of their allocation and "set it aside" for training for the teachers who weren't highly qualified. What did the federal government say was a Highly Qualified Teacher (HQT)? It left it up to each state. New York identified HQT teachers as: having a bachelor degree and teaching certification. For many districts, especially small and rural ones, having a HQT in every classroom is difficult if not impossible. In urban schools, the need for bilingual teachers who are certified as well is often an example of a high demand, low supply market.

Step 2: is the district classified as in accountable status? If yes, it needs to set aside 10 % of your federal money to allow students to get tutoring after school (called supplemental education services or ses). Not a bad idea-right? In theory SES should help students, except it didn't. Most tutoring providers were not very good. Many were teachers themselves who set up shop. Others were on-line providers or group tutoring providers. Most SES providers were for profit groups who in many instances charged a huge amount per student, and many students did not benefit. In rural locations, some schools had no one willing to provide the SES tutoring. The district also had to set aside 10% of the school funds to finance professional development that was targeted to get the school out of accountability. If the entire district was in accountability, then 10% of the entire district's money had to be set aside for professional development. If it were a large enough district, then there was a requirement to set aside 10% of the district's federal money to allow students to transfer into a school in good standing in the district. In the Northern United States, a court case said that districts were not forced to accept students from out of district (Holme, Finnigan & Diem, 2016). Many parents and districts often engaged in conflict over district boundaries, especially near New York City. The parents wanted to send their child to a different school than the boundaries allowed, so many appeals to the Commissioner of Education happened over residency determinations. In New York, a parent cannot cross district lines unless the receiving school agrees or the parents pay tuition. So let us review the state's (and our team's role) in school improvement money:

5% if all teachers not qualified

10% for professional development

10% for school choice

10% for Supplemental Education Services (tutoring)

At least 35% of a school district's money if they are in

accountability was assigned to programs that would not directly help students. To review: Title I funding is to help students, especially the most at risk due to poverty.

Then the schools needed to identify improvement plans—called CEPS or comprehensive education plans. The plans would outline how the schools were going to meet the standards set by the Board of Regents for elementary testing, in English Language Arts, math and science. Further accountability measures included tests in middle school ELA and math and science. Then, high school ELA and math, and tests were required. High school Social Studies and science tests were included under the graduation rate accountability score. Schools needed to meet a minimum percentage of graduates and two social studies exams; US History and Government and Global History and Geography were required as part of graduation pathways. Most of the plans contained details about how administrators would be more accountable by visiting teachers' classrooms more often. In many instances the plans would include teams to study data from the state tests regularly. Other districts would focus on professional development sessions after school, on weekends, or over the summer.

The state would also give schools help by offering regional technical assistance networks. These centers were designed to help schools with strategic planning, resource identification, and distribution and coaching for teachers and administrators. What I found was that many of the technical assistance center staffers were in a bit of a quandary. These dedicated professionals often saw the centers as a stepping stone on a journey, and the "field based" administrators were leery that their assistance was not field tested. I discovered that there was no shortage for districts who needed help with school improvement. State Ed had a number of other networks providing "help to districts" from monitors (Title I, Special Education) to curriculum and instruction experts from the Office of Curriculum and Instruction.

The levels of technical assistance for the districts in the form of support networks were overwhelming. One school administrator would have two state officials, and up to 10 BOCES support staff there to help the one person make "change." These support groups were loosely coordinated by the School Improvement Officer who would call together all the partners at a table once a quarter to discuss what the networks were doing to help the schools. These two hour meetings would "highlight" the issues facing the district, as all the networks viewed the same issue. I often joked I was leading a half a million dollar meeting that moved so slowly. To our greatest faults, at the beginning, we never included the district administrators at these meetings. These network meetings usually devolved into people upset about how the districts weren't using their resources and asking, "What's our role?" Maybe it was my impatient 29-year old self, but I could not stand not getting work done. I wanted to see the districts changed and helped. I believed that we were responsible for raising the knowledge, skill and opportunity for all citizens of New York, not just getting paid a lot.

So there is this counter intuitive way of helping schools: take away money and add a ton of help to overwhelmed administrators who did not know how to use, or prioritize the competing demands on their time. It was ironic that the mission of our support teams was to raise the internal capacity of school districts. Capacity is a fancy leaderspeak work for human capital—or the ability to deal with your own problems! State Ed, with its bureaucracy, liked to let local schools fix their own problems—unless the public and media created a firestorm that forced the State Education Department to act.

The reason I was hired was one small district made famous by Kozol's (2012) book on the segregated state of American Schools. This small one-mile square school district on Long Island is a source of sorrow for the residents, the state, and many others. The district has been the center of turmoil over the years, first as rapid expansion led to overcrowding, and then declining resources as the community suffered from increased poverty. The system became subject to increased state oversight as its buildings began to crumble and become unstable. Additionally, the state and federal auditors found the district wasn't spending money according to regulations. School performance declined at the elementary and secondary level. Students were not graduating, test performance was low level, and the dropout rate was one of the worst in the State. The Education Department declared not just the high school, but the entire district under registration review. Board of Education in-fighting and problems with elections resulted in a number of appeals to the Commissioner of Education. As members of the Board increasingly found collaboration difficult, and administrators left regularly, the Legislature issued an order dismissing the Board of Education, directing the State Education Department to take over the district and monitor its actions. The *New York Times* and *Newsday* of Long Island urged state action as money, social, racial, and achievement issues drove the future of the hamlet and community further away from the goal of raising the knowledge and skills of the citizens in the state of New York.

As I joined the Department, the district was again the subject of state and Regents oversight. One liaison on the team held the sole assignment of monitoring the district. He was the coordinating liaison for just one district. A 2600 student district with multiple administrators was overseen by one liaison. To put that in perspective, large districts had to share liaisons among multiple districts. The state was putting huge resources into monitoring the one district, including the appointment of a fiscal monitor and a Board of Education monitor. My job was to help pick up the oversight for the rest of the down state, non-New York City Schools. A few of the highly segregated suburban school districts required enhanced monitoring for academic and fiscal accountability.

In late fall, the Commissioner of Education, Richard Mills, and the Chancellor of the Board of Regents, William Bennett, requested a team of SED staff go to the district and discover the state of the schools. This team was massive. Almost 30 members of the State Education Department were sent to the one district to conduct a comprehensive examination of the state of the district.

The team left Sunday night and encamped in a hotel. From this base of operations, we each went to a different school/district office location to review documents, observe classrooms, interview faculty, staff, and students. Every school in the district was observed for three days. For me, a rookie, this was an overwhelming and in some ways disturbing experience. Having grown up in the sheltered suburb of Hamburg, NY, and having taught in small rural districts, I could not believe the issues I observed in the district. The elementary school I observed was half shuttered, and the majority of students were in trailers. The building was molded, and structurally unsound. Yet the Board and the Community could not agree on the construction of a new school. At the middle-high school, the building looked as if it had suffered battle wounds from a conflict zone. The kids and staff in the district were in buildings that looked like they were from a war zone.

When we met the principal, a nice, older woman, you got the sense she cared about the kids. From the south, with a thick southern accent, the principal was proud of what her students did accomplish while they attended an area of salutary educational neglect by the community, the district, and the state. Salutary neglect was the British policy towards the American Colonies in the 1600-1700s. Essentially, the British government left the colonies alone, as long as materials and money flowed home. The principal was so proud of the singing ability of her students, and the artistic expression which flowed from their creative centers. She showed us her chorus of students who sang "Lift Every Voice and Sing" by Johnson (2019). She then escorted the state education department monitors to the gym and had her dance team performed a routine. While my SED mentor and the Special Education monitor and I looked on, the principal escorted us everywhere around the building that still existed and showed us what I would consider extracurriculars and co-curriculars. She was so proud of what her students did outside of the classroom.

Before lunch, I asked my SED mentor when we would see the classroom. His words still haunt me: "Let her have this joy, the classroom is her brutal truth." My mentor, with a PhD, has served as a building principal overseas. He has expertise in urban environments, teaching at-risk students, and career and technical education. A wise man now retired, his witticisms carried me and his wise counsel guided me to realize that many educators are hard workers in impossible systems. Many are surrounded by situations that no professional would tolerate. They are missionaries hoping and striving to right wrongs inflicted on many repressed communities. These educators are well educated, but many have had to turn to religious faith, because the secular system is broken beyond repair.

As we entered the classroom at the elementary school, I found the honest truth of education in the school to be worse than the written word and reports. In some classrooms, there was nothing on the walls. The teacher sat at their desk and had students work on worksheets. There were no colorful posters up, no over packed classroom libraries. Other times, I saw students waiting in line in the hallway—the teacher trying to wrangle squirmy 2nd graders into a straight line so they could walk the halls quietly and organized. In a third room, there was work up on the wall that had been incorrectly marked. Spelling in fifth grade should have some modicum of presence, but here, it was absent. The crowded portables had that humid smell to them, the dank feeling of too much water in the air. The physical structure of these temporary classrooms looked as if they too were at the end of their physical lives. Not more than 200 feet away stood the brick and mortar school—closed due to physical safety issues.

There was one classroom that impressed me. A former lawyer gave up her practice and became a 6th grade teacher. She would organize "court" each day, and have students present to her in judge's robes some aspect of learning they would cover. A "prosecutor" or a "defense" expert would present a grammar case, or social studies fact case, or a science principle case, and the students in teams would have to argue for or against that item. The rest of the class acted as a jury, deciding if the information presented was correct or incorrect. This teacher demonstrated a number of key attributes that I would hold to be the source of successful instruction.

First, she made the children feel agency in the classroom. The students were in control of their learning, and the task was accomplished in an engaging way that no child was left outside the classroom learning. Second, she demonstrated engagement with her students. They knew that she cared for them as scholars and as individuals. Third, she role modeled successful career goals for students from minority and poor communities. She made the students believe. Fourth, she was prepared for classroom experiences. Her lesson plans were well thought out, achieved, and exceeded state standards, and most importantly, taught students to self- monitor and take responsibility for their own learning. The physical classroom was set up in a semicircle, with a carpet in the center of the floor and a riot of colorful posters and displays in the classroom. This teacher spent a lot of her own money to make the classroom covered in color. Not only that, but her students' work was displayed prominently around the room. There were a number of essays, experiment reports, maps, and math problems displayed which showed visitors and students alike how proud of their work the class and teacher were. To this day, over a decade later, I still think the classroom of the judge was one of the best I ever saw.

After three solid days of seeing the elementary school inside and out, I could see how the school suffered from a split teaching faculty. Some loved their jobs, and believed that all children could learn and they would, dammit, do their best to not only lift every voice, but lift every child. Other teachers tried but were exhausted. They did what was needed, but the constant test prep and textbook fed lessons were compliance in nature. No more, no less to meet what the administrator wanted to ensure no disciplinary actions would emerge. The third group foundered. They foundered because they did not know how to teach. These teachers did not know how to plan the lesson. They could not use data to change lessons. They were unaware of connections across the curriculum that would tie together the materials students were supposed to learn.

The textbook was their lifeline for everything. They were unaware of state documents on curriculum and instruction. They did not know about test question samplers. The internet and technology wasn't used effectively or efficiently. For this group of teachers, a smart board was a glorified chalkboard, used as a screen to project an overhead image from an overhead machine. This group needed mentoring, and coaching, and someone to show the teachers how to find materials and keep up with systematic changes.

The fourth, and finally the last group were the abusers of the system. They were experienced, and quite often with a grudge on their shoulder. They felt slighted for some reason. This group made it clear to the state monitors the axe needed grinding. The administration didn't like them. Or they didn't want to teach that grade level. They hated the school they were in, or felt that the kids and their parents didn't care. They worked for the money, and often believed that retirement was due to them, even if it was 20 years away. They did not seek out whatever wasn't given to them. They made kids do problems from a book, or handed out worksheets. When a state monitor conducted interviews with the teachers concerning their students, their response was telling. Asked about their class, they would respond: "their poor, they are slow, what do you expect." Other times, this group would say "the administration is so incompetent, I don't know how they got their jobs." When talking to SED liaisons like me, this group of teachers demonstrated a profound lack of knowledge and understanding of some real basics in education. Many teachers in this group never went to conferences, they never volunteered for committees. They never implemented Class Wide or School Wide

Behavior Intervention systems. They had no knowledge of the grade level or other committee work being done. Frequently they arrived last and left first. This group often cited the contract as a reason for not doing something: "Why should I stay late, they don't pay me. It's against the contract." For a district in state take over, these were some of the largest oppositional points to any change that could be made in the district.

I want to pause, and say clearly, the system let these teachers down, yes. I also want to say that I value the boundaries established within professional contracts. I do not agree with the way in which these adults had given up on students. A small group of adults, to be sure, but a really hurtful group nonetheless.

My experience was not the first time the district had been reviewed. Within a 10 year span of time (1990s-2000s), the District had been investigated numerous times. It had been reviewed by multiple numbers of outside experts. Each time, three themes emerged: leadership was weak, classroom instruction was rote, and the general organization of all aspects of education were undeveloped. We said the same thing: almost 30 staff investigated over one week. Looking at reports created since the 1980s, they all said the same thing. Each time phrases such as "might" or "may" or "could" entered their way into reports, never "must" or"should `` or"are required to" so that the state would not be perceived as telling a school what to do. The public required accountability; our internal structure shied away from orders. The only time our department became insistent on a path, strongly worded directives, or "Commissioner's Orders" were issued to school districts in the name of the Commissioner. These legally binding directives had force of law, and if ignored, would result in Board member's removals. Roosevelt had received Commissioner's orders in the past and ignored them. Hence, the removal of the Board by State Ed.

When we returned home, our staff worked on the reports, summarizing the findings of our visit. A report was issued to the

Board of Regents about what the team found. The SED monitor and the team continued to meet with the district administration off site. It was an exercise that I would engage in numerous times over my seven years at the Department.

After the visit to the district, it was decided the time had arrived for me to monitor my own district. So a larger, multicultural district was selected as my district. Not knowing what to expect sent a shiver of anticipation down my spine. When we arrived at my newly assigned big district, our meeting included every school administrator at the district level and all of the principals and most assistant principals from the schools identified as low performing. Joining us were the support network personnel. There must have been a half a million dollars in salary alone in that room—probably more. The district had just hired a new interim superintendent to serve as the district looked to hire a permanent one after the long-time superintendent had retired. This district is huge, and as such had an extraordinary number of Directors. Coming in at almost 20,000 children, the big district is one of the largest in New York State. A suburban community that has morphed into an inner ring suburb,the big district was once an award-winning district. It still is, if you count its art, music and some Advanced Placement programs.

The district had fallen on hard times academically, with the district identified as in need of improvement. Its high school, full of 3600 students grades 10-12, was in corrective action, the middle stage of accountability. All four middle schools were deep in accountability, and some of the elementary schools were starting to appear on the accountability list. As we met with the administration and support teams, I got the sense from my mentor that this district had massive concerns. Not so much as the smaller district we had visited, but a number. The Superintendent had yet to receive the transfer of federal aid for the Consolidated Application, or the Schools in Need of Improvement (1003a) money. To give you an idea, the big district received 3 million dollars from the federal government for Title I alone, and another $80,000 for school improvement. All told, federal money flowing into this big district was a large chunk of change. Our itinerary for the next day was to visit the middle and high schools together. Stopping at each of the five buildings, I was struck with some niceties and some good teaching in the district. I was also impressed with how hard the administrators and teachers were working with their students to help them be successful. When we left the big district to go back to Albany, I thought that I'd be able to work with the place.

My first task when I arrived back at Albany was to ensure the Title I application and School Improvement grant got approved as soon as possible. When I found the grant, it was piled with other district grants. So I went about the task of reviewing the narrative, designed as a plan to describe what the money was used for to the state and any future federal auditors. My next task was to check the budget to ensure it complied with the federal requirements for set asides. I noticed that the district wasn't spending all of the Title I budget. I couldn't understand why. They were leaving money in the roll over part of the budget, which allows districts to keep unspent funds to the next year and then pad the budget a little more. What I didn't realize, and was made painfully clear to me later was a little known fact: The feds only issue preliminary allocations. Later, in January or February, they pull back some of the money to make "adjustments." I had made a $150,000 dollar a year administrator make changes on the budget for nothing. I learned a huge lesson that day: be as careful as possible, the State's reputation was not great in the field.

I found many admins and teachers thought SED employees were stupid, lazy and incompetent. The old saying went "Hi, I'm from State Ed, and I'm here to help." More often than not it wasn't the truth. SED imposed a number of regulations on schools, or what was worse, made administrators and teachers comply with stupid rules and regs which made no sense out in the "field." It pained me. As an Eagle Scout I wanted "to help other people at all times..." including students who were at no fault of their own missing out on educational opportunities. When districts couldn't get access to federal funds, then educational programs were started, teachers weren't hired, materials and supplies weren't purchased. While SED did not intentionally hold up funds, we often could not approve them timely either.

So next time I went to Long Island, I talked to the superintendent about emailing me a copy of the application ahead of time or going over the document in the summer while at the building, and making sure the compliance part was done so I could approve the document when the original hit my desk. I also worked very closely with Grants Finance to ensure High Priority district applications, such as those in accountability would be expedited to the reviewers. Our processes and systems were leaking because they were so dependent on people, and when there aren't enough people, then the system doesn't always work. For perspective, years of state budget difficulties had reduced the number of folks to a skeleton crew. Once entire bureaus stood ready to help. Now, one person oversees all the social studies curriculum for the entire state.

Later that year, I was asked to join one of my teammates in preparing for a School Under Registration Review. The State had, starting in the 1980s, identified the worst performing schools in an effort to force (at that time) city school districts to do something. These SURR schools were the worst in the state—often the bottom 5% on any measure of achievement. The school was then subjected to a week-long visit by State Education Department officials, who would examine every aspect of the school. This process was intense. If the school did not improve, then the state could withdraw its registration, and the program would need to close.

The district identified was almost 100% underrepresented students. The tax base had eroded, and there was no room to rebuild or retrofit in the community. There is a large dump near the community. The residents and its schools are the only thing, beside churches, which keep the hamlet running.

A School Under Registration Review process starts with SED

notifying the school district Board of Education and administration that the school may be identified. The District is then allowed to rebut and appeal that decision. Once the appeal is over, the Commissioner releases a list to the press. Local newspapers often report on this announcement. Frequently it makes the TV media as well. The Department then assigns one of the BOCES District Superintendents to name a team of experts and work with an SED employee to establish a visit to the school district. The SED liaison and the DS send the protocol to the District, establish the date of the visit, and communicate with the District to ensure the school understands the severity of the visit. Once this happens, the SED liaison is sent to the school and district to meet with the administrative team, the faculty and staff, and parents to discuss what the designation means, and what the process will entail. These are often intense meetings, and quite commonly the faculty and staff are very hostile. After all, the State just told the entire school community that they are failing the children entrusted to their care.

After a couple of weeks, the team, led by the BOCES District Superintendent, arrives on a Sunday to begin planning the visitations. A full report must be issued orally to the school on friday. These meetings for logistics will discuss what each person's role will be for the event. Often documents are handed out. Quite frequently, we are reminded of the sensitive nature of the visit. One time, a SURR team member on a visit threw draft notes away in their hotel trash, and the contents were leaked to the newspaper while the visit was happening. Needless to say, SURR visit findings are not pretty, and often cast the staff and school leadership in a less than positive light.

First thing Monday morning, before the students even arrived, the team made its way to the school to watch as children entered the building. We see how the staff does or does not interact with the students. We watch how the students interact with each other. Often the SED team members are the only white faces in the crowd of students. After watching the students enter, the DS, along with the rest of the team, will meet with the school administrators. This meeting describes the course of the visit, including classroom visits, document reviews, interviews with teachers, and focus groups with students. We cannot officially "observe teachers" because this is often, in their contracts, an official supervision and management process with repercussions for employment.

Our visit to a SURR school quite often includes an examination of the teaching and learning, curriculum, assessment and classroom environment of the school. The team will further examine the leadership, use of data, and state of the building. We often investigate safety, parental engagement, and extra-curricular offerings. A SURR visit starts at the front sign and ends once we have seen everything. It is in-depth and intrusive, but often necessary to ferret out what goes on. I have found after conducting multiple SURR visits, and other school improvement visits, that many schools that are struggling will try and stage manage the visitors as much as possible. They will hide what areas they are most ashamed of from the SED team. Sometimes this comes as a passive aggressive act of not including all information ahead of time. Usually bell schedules, teacher class assignments, and curriculum documents were not included in the materials sent up ahead of time. Teachers would sometimes call out sick during our visits. Other times, lesson plans were not made available during the visit for review. I always personally enjoyed it when a teacher scheduled a video or a test during the review. Other times during visits, teachers, administrators and staff would be super helpful. They would give us hints about where to look for the skeletons in the closet. They would show us exactly which teachers were the "problem children" or they would lead us to stars, who the local teaching staff wanted to single out for praise but we could not. It wasn't impartial or state like.

The best part of the visit was listening to the students, who would tell adults three and four times their age, with letters after their names, what exactly was wrong with the school and how to fix it. It was an exhilarating moment to see a young, often disenfranchised student not only hold their own, but enthrall so called educational experts. And their honesty was born of a frustration of having to live through mediocrity or failure. The students voiced frustration at their peers, for "throwing away their shot." They were angry that classroom materials assigned to them were underwhelming, and often significantly behind standards and expectations for the grade level.

On this particular visit you could see the seams and frayed edges at all areas of the school. The principal, a nice young guy who was trying so hard to help the school, looked like he was going to have a medical crisis. Later the lead on the visit told us during the interview the principal was relieved to hear he wasn't crazy, and there really were problems in the school which needed addressing. For one, this leader, who was held accountable for everything in his school, had no say over who was placed in the building due to issues beyond his control. Second, he had no control over disciplining children, because that task was sent to a hearing officer. Third, he had no control over his budget. Those decisions were made at the District office. When you place so much responsibility, but allow so little autonomy, you are creating failure and setting people up for a mental and physical health crisis.

The district had a growing immigrant population which needed servicing, and the teachers there were not prepared to help. The technical assistance group charged with going into the school to help couldn't always. Sometimes, they confessed, they were afraid of the boisterous nature of the students. You were also hit hard with how disengaged many of the teachers were in the school. For these adults, the overwhelming nature of the dysfunction had created an unsafe zone, and survival was the only place to focus.

As interviews progressed, I began to ask their undergraduate school and major, as well as years teaching. Many had previously served in New York City. Some had been fired or resigned from other suburban Long Island districts. Many had attended less than prestigious colleges. They had majored in a subject other than their discipline which they were teaching. Often those teachers had generalist degrees—psychology or humanities. Rarely did they have a master's degree in their field. Many had studied general education, or educational administration. Some had degrees in special education, but weren't implementing their learnings in the classroom. Almost all of the teachers could not identify what they were proud of in the district. They were clear what was wrong. They felt unsupported. They wanted to know why more kids weren't in special education or disciplined out of their classroom. They felt angered that the salaries among the administrators were so high, and yet they lacked textbooks.

I often wonder why, in this age of the internet (starting with my undergraduate career in 1995), textbooks are still a fall back for many teachers. Most teachers fail to use those really expensive teaching aids that come with textbooks—the guide, documents, maps, differentiated learning, overhead projectors, CD Roms and DVDs. Half the time the packets include lessons, quizzes, tests, and standards alignment charts. The publisher has done all of your work for you. All you need to do is plug and play. Additionally, the internet has the resources you need for a pretty robust curriculum. These open education resources and sites which include free materials have exploded. Documents are online. They are free. Lesson ideas are online. They are free. Many classrooms are now equipped with a Smartboard, or with a projector which attaches to a computer. Hell, almost all of the kids have phones that are so advanced that we don't need computers in the classroom anymore—they bring their own!

I also never understood why teachers never liked to get feedback on their lessons. Yes I know it's difficult to hear you weren't perfect. I always became nervous about the principal's feedback, but I was young and inexperienced. Honestly, the only way to improve is with lesson studies. Japanese teachers study and support each other in lesson planning and data analytics all of the time (Chokshi & Fernandez, 2004). The Finns apparently do so much collegial conversation that the US is sending waves of teachers and researchers there (Sahlberg, 2007). The US education system does not like what it perceives as waste—the idea that a teacher not teaching during the day is a waste of money. Instead, teachers who don't try to improve their craft keep using the same lessons year after year for decades. The lesson is the roadmap for the trip, and I understand planning is hard work. Many of the teachers at our school under registration review did not reflect on their lessons or their crafts. They instead handed out worksheets. Reams and books worth of worksheets, which are disposed of after class, or stuffed into lockers, or thrown around the school because students aren't challenged by the worksheets, or see the purpose in filling the worksheet out.

At the end of the week, the team needed to present our findings and recommendations to the school, the district, and the superintendent. What I remember most was the hostility from the superintendent. I also remember the hostility from the staff. We took no questions, we provided no clarification. The District Superintendent leading the survey spoke. And then the SED liaison was left to try and work with the group who hated the visit. Again, we recommended that the district and the teachers and the school administration should do something. We found the teaching lacked rigor. We found the curriculum lacked alignment. We found the school did not utilize data to inform instruction. There were issues with resource allocation. Staffing turnover was high. The physical facilities were in need of renovation. And all of this while the school had been identified multiple times in the past as a SURR. In fact, the district had so many issues that the Department had issued a performance plan which held the school district and board of education accountable for basic tasks, like submitting plans and grants on time. And yet with all that human resources, and all of the monitoring, and accountability, the district was still one of the lowest performing in the state.

That was just my first year—and it got more intensive and interesting from there.

REFLECTIONS:

- How do you handle change when the ethics and practices don't quite align with your personal belief system?
- If you could propose a sweeping systematic change for education, what would this be and why?

POLICY AND PROFESSIONAL CHANGE

This chapter focuses on my internal growth, and my realization that reality does not match the ideal. I tell some stories specifically about how policy is conceived, enacted, and communicated. A true reflection on education in a large state, realizing that the right or wrong choice impacts students.

Guiding question: How do you deal with reality versus ideal?

Year two at the State Education Department became a study in how the "sausage" of government is really made. I spent that summer working with the "low priority schools" in my assigned region. My goal was simple: prove I was really there to help, hoping to create a bond with staff members as they were implementing small school improvement grants in summer school sessions. I met amazing people doing wonderful work for children. They honestly believed that the work which they were undertaking was the "right work." The ethos shown in how they tackled summer school, and the enthusiastic nature of their engagement with children. What is odd was the number of University at Buffalo alumni in the area who wanted to go back to Buffalo. So many times Buffalo gets a bad rap for its weather, but so many folks loved the climate, the culture, the food, and the vibrant scene which was playing out.

When we entered the fall, and were beginning to plan for consolidated application reviews, I found myself reviewing my own districts I oversaw, but taking an increasing load from others. Later, as the legislative session was heating up, we heard rumors of an article 57, then chapter 57, that was going to change how we did business in the state with schools in trouble. The law which finally passed is now known as "Contract for Excellence" and took state aid increases and tied the extra money to a series of steps a district in accountability had to take to spend that money on required actions.

The legislation directed districts to spend the extra state aid, normally given without strings, according to specified reform efforts. Schools could implement one of five options:

- class-size reduction
- teacher and principal quality
- full-day pre-K and kindergarten
- longer school day
- middle and high school restructuring

Within these five areas, school districts were supposed to dedicate the new money to help improve the academic performance of all their students. As the state monitors, we needed to ensure that the districts had a well thought out plan for spending the additional monies. Many of the districts were searching for ways to ensure that the new money could be used as a way to keep in place projects which were ending, and they were beginning to feel in 2007 the earliest stages of the Great Recession.

New York is dependent on collected tax revenues from the Wall Street world. Most of the state's taxes emerge from income taxes which are levied on people's wages. This also includes the significant bonuses that the Wall Street brokerage firms give at the end of the year. As Wall Street sneezes, the state catches cold. The state was beginning to experience pneumonia. In the upstate area, the region north of Orange and Dutchess county, the economy still had not recovered from the 1970s, and the deindustrialization of the region. Continued outflow of residents put some communities into an epic death spiral. For some areas, like Utica, Rochester, Buffalo, Schenectady, and Syracuse, immigrants and refugees from around the world were flooding into their cities—posing additional problems for schools who could not cope with their needs and the lagging funding which the federal government would give to these schools. A mess was brewing in many areas of the state.

Collaboratively and across offices, we developed monitoring tools for Contract for Excellence, or C4E monies so the districts would be in compliance. We would work closely with other offices as well to examine what school districts were doing in a select number of schools to ensure that the programs were being carried out within the spirit and letter of the law. As the summer moved into fall, our office was gifted with hiring a number of new people, doubling our team's size. We also began to lose members to retirement. The State Comptroller's office wanted to replace necessary hires only, so as the "old money" Title I funded people left, only "new money" C4E people would be hired on. There were two sets of C4E people hired, the experienced Associate positions, and the newly hired Assistant positions. So some of the greatest staff I came to work with were brought into SED at this hiring moment. It was a real shot of fresh ideas to a department which hadn't seen major staffing increases in years.

As we developed the monitoring tools for the C4E, I was introduced to our New York City based school improvement team. Many of these people had done yeoman's work in the City and had pioneered New York's first school improvement wave, the School Under Registration Review Process. The SURR process emerged out of a need to address some of the worst schools in the nation. It was an intensive process which involved in-depth data analysis of the schools identified as the lowest performing in the state. A high stress and thorough investigation of the schools often reveal structural issues with how the district is run, how the building is managed, and how teachers are usually concerned with survival.

As we worked together developing the protocols to ensure that the C4E money was spent by regulation, I found myself visiting the big district's elementary schools. Inside those elementary schools were very dedicated teachers, and a whole new world. Quite a few students were from the south and central American nations. They were learning English at the same time they were learning academic subjects.They were also struggling with poverty, and in many cases the attendant issues associated with crime in their community. Many of the teachers were creative and thought provoking. They tried hard to ensure the base level of Maslow's hierarchy of needs was met. You remember— the basics like safety, food, and shelter. Often though, the needs of their students were years behind their grade level. Many couldn't read in the special education subpopulation. Overall, the schools spent their money well, but many basic things were needed— such as building reconstruction, technology upgrades and, in some instances, the faculty needed a mental break. It is intensive working with students for 180 days, for 7 hours a day.

I was also asked to go on a monitoring trip to two smaller cities in the Hudson Valley and Central New York. Additional duties included regularly scheduled visits to schools and districts for Title I monitoring. I had the opportunity to visit a large urban district. I was beginning to work with districts which I had responsibility on paper for, but also later on large visits to schools and districts that I would assume responsibility for. In a number of those rural districts, the poverty was obvious to anyone who had eyes and ears.

Some of the students in those communities were living in conditions which boggled the mind. Having lived in Norwich previously, I had the unique opportunity to return back to the school and see what was going on in the district. There are so many social and economic issues that impact small city schools—and because they do not have critical mass, help is often not forthcoming. In some of the most rural counties of New York, poverty and lack of job opportunities are stealing kids' futures. Sherman and Sage (2011) as well as Duncan (1999), have written on the issues faced in rural resource extraction communities. Carr and Kefalas (2009), in their book *Hollowing Out the Middle* found a mismatch between the community's needs and the curriculum. Mike Corbett (2007), one of the leading scholars on the subject, demonstrated convincingly that rural areas and their school systems are often in conflict. Why do schools educate students to leave? Why haven't more place-based curricular projects been implemented? It often starts with the monopolies by the reformers. Many times teachers believe that workbooks or textbooks are the curriculum.

The voices of new scholars are adding great research to our knowledge, with Thier, et al (2021) finding that rural Northeast United States communities have been largely ignored by "peer reviewed" research. Julia Miller (2021), a researcher after my own heart (but way SMARTER!), examined how state policies on consolidation rip the heart out of local communities and destroy them for good. Chea Parton (2021) took an in-depth look at rural English educators, and how there are few well known resources for place-based curriculum. Rachel Chamberlain (2020) examined how some shared superintendents negotiate between districts and can reduce the "us versus them" mentalities. My own dissertation (2020) and book (2020) examined how rural areas were in constant rear guard action, as the state resource decline was melding with decreasing resources.

In the spring of that year, after all of our new people were hired, I led a large team of SED staff to a medium-sized district in my assigned region to conduct a Title I audit. This audit would be the end of the sitting superintendent's work, and the introduction of a new one. With the new superintendent, my SED partner and I would for the next three years work closely together to ensure that the school district began to make a turn into higher achievement. We worked to see all of the elementary, intermediate, middle, and high schools. We asked important and hard questions about the district's financial spending patterns and how the district could build on what was working. JS is near and dear to my heart, and I want to protect her privacy. We worked in tandem with the superintendent, visited the schools and showed we were a united force, the school, the state, and special ed. The principals of the district enjoyed our visits, and found we were able to help them identify and create strong plans designed to improve the school. They appreciated our presentations and insights into what was working, what wasn't working, and steps to make changes. We highlighted the good, not good, and how to get there.

Later that year, in the spring, I was asked to lead a SURR visit to A Large URBAN District. Here I met Dr. Mike O and his team from the local BOCES. A phenomenal group of people, the work we did in the A Large URBAN District allowed the superintendent to begin enacting plans to try and transform some of the lowest achieving schools in the state. The Large URBAN District suffers from massive poverty. It is one of the poorest cities in the United States. As the city deindustrialized, gone were the days of many large and formerly wealthy companies, and many of the first happenings in the US. When you look at the city, it was the home of a famous sufferagette There was a strong abolitionist newspaper which was directly responsible for educating the public about the horrors of slavery. A major scholarly book read by many discusses the beginnings of the "burnt over district" along the Erie Canal in the region. Home to the flour mills along the river, brewing companies, and the specific flower festival, the region has amazing culture and festive events. To its west, a village exists which is home to a tasty dessert. A large rural history museum holds a living history visitors village which chronicles everyday life in the time period in the area. To the south, in another community, a large national university began as a secondary school, as another profoundly scholarly work recounts. All along the great lake, among the apple trees and farms, you see historic signs reminding visitors of the significance of this area during the War of 1812. The city is home to museums, universities, art museums, and a whole host of attractions.

The Large URBAN District has undergone a number of reform attempts over the past 40 years. The district looked to its neighbors for an urban-suburban exchange program. This reform attempt allowed a limited number of city children an opportunity to enroll in a suburban school district. A suburban child, if their family so chose, could enroll in a city school. A second major reform effort the district tried involved a small schools movement that a major educational foundation funded. As schools, especially high schools were identified in need of improvement, the same educational foundation gave the district money to break the large 1000+ student buildings into small learning communities. Other reform efforts included transitioning children between 7-12 and K-8 buildings. Depending on the goals, the idea of a 7-12 building insists that high school students will serve as role models for middle school students. In a K-8 building, the idea is to shield children from the high school children. The research also suggests that the constant transitions in high schools between subjects and rooms can interrupt the flow of the day. By reducing the exposure to bad behavior from older students, and keeping students in supportive teams, research suggests dropping out can be forestalled or eliminated (Lehr *et al*, 2003).

The final reform the Large URBAN District was subject to were the charter schools. Thankfully, charter mania had not swept that city like it had in Albany, NYC or Buffalo, NY city schools. In the early 2000s, there were charter schools in the city, but not too many. Many children in the schools attended elementary schools in the city school district and then transferred to a charter school if they could for middle and high school. The uniforms, the structured classrooms, and the scripted lessons echoed in many closed Catholic schools which had been converted into charter schools. Many teachers in the charter schools had graduated from college and held a liberal arts degree. This model was similar to what Teach for America in New York City used for their teacher recruitment model.

It was interesting to note the SURR visits to both the smaller suburban district and The Large URBAN District revealed a number of continuing problems in resource starved education. The first hand observations I made on those two SURR visits reminded me one of the strongest issues which needs addressing but is ignored by the structure is teacher burnout (see Froelich, 2020. There has been a number of studies linking the effects of poverty to issues students and families face. But we need to remember the teachers as well. As researchers have pointed out, most teachers come from and wish to teach in homogeneous and middle class districts. In an urban environment, or a rural area, this may be the first time the teacher, as a person, is facing such a wide level of poverty and the effects on students.

How could the team tell the teachers were burned out? With some it was quite easy—the physical manifestations of burn-out are evident. Physically looking exhausted is one key identifier. The second is the mental signs of stress, the ways in which small, almost routine, matter of fact activities were overwhelming. Third indicator is attendance. For a number of SURR school teachers, absenteeism was high. Finally, the teachers had given up. For some who had given up, these actions included going through the motions. For a number of staff members, going through the motions meant using worksheets or dittos. They might lecture at the class, not even to the class. Quite often, instruction wasn't engaging, and rather basic.

For others, the side hustle became the main hustle. In one building, I witnessed a teacher using an overhead to project a lesson onto a turned off smart board. When interviewed later he said that he was busy running his personal training business. Another teacher in the building owned a catering business. They had given up on the students placed in front of them because the system had made it too difficult to continue. The two focused on their own needs at the expense of their students. Again, a small number, but damning nonetheless.

In moving throughout the SURR building, it was easy to see how beaten up many of the staff members felt about their world. The system had broken them by continuously creating churn. To the average American, a teacher is hired, receives summer breaks, and is tenured into a lifelong job. The political rhetoric is demanding people attack their educational institutions as sources of "liberalism" and "civilized decay" without understanding what eroding support for public education has done (Cervone, 2017). In those SURR schools, the faculty are often bumped every year by opening and closing campuses around the city. Other problems occur when budget projections are off by central administrators. Every year at least 10% of the staff at the Large URBAN School are dismissed for reduction in force reasons. Their positions are abolished, and they are placed on a recall list. The list services the district, not just the school, and quite often the teachers are placed poorly or last minute. In many instances, the Large URBAN District will have temporary assignments teaching until late October.

For the kids in these high poverty (70%+) schools, a teacher may be the only adult who cares for them. Research shows that an adult at school is a critical need for students in poverty to find success. When a school is in trouble, it is usually the build-up of decades of problems that the system inflicts on students, staff, and admins, as well as students. On the flip side, I saw some teachers act as bullies towards well meaning administrators. They would willfully fail to follow common decency and would engage in active subterfuge. It was their understanding that the kids could not do, the administration would not do, and so mentally, they were done.

In Evan's book *The Human Side of School Change* (1996), the psychologist author raises an extraordinarily interesting point. People change mindsets when they enter a situation requiring change. The initial stage sees the person negatively react against the chaos and poor environment. The individual works in a dedicated and urgent way to make changes to the surrounding situation. They advocate, they strategize, and they fight. As their energy begins to flag, and the situation remains the same, the people move into a stage of apathy and self-survival. The individual realizes that they have no power or control over the situation and cannot make a change. They cannot make things better. They cannot influence events. They need to survive. They need to ensure that their person is safe. Maslow's pyramid is broken down to the foundation stones. After some time in the situation, a Stockholm Syndrome event changes the person into an owner of the mess. Now instead of denying involvement, a person who has been in a failing school for three or more years now has ownership. They are part of the problem. The individual has created, however small, a small part of the continued existence and must own it. During this time, Evans (1996) mentions the rationalization done to protect a person's ego. For some, it is an unflagging belief they tried their best, but weren't good enough. Others believe that they made change, it just didn't stick. Or they made significant changes in the area which they have control over. The school is in chaos, my classroom is controlled.

It was during this timeframe I began to hear about "courageous conversations" (Mireles-Rios & Becchio, 2018). Talking with some school superintendents, and with retired administrators, a courageous conversation is one that an administrator has with an underperforming teacher. It is also a conversation around areas that make us uncomfortable, such as racism, classism, and sexism. The central point for many education based conversations was to call underperforming teachers out and help them by motivating them to see the errors of their ways. This business strategy—or coaching—has recently made the rounds throughout educational circles. Books, seminars, webinars, and a whole host of events and ink have been devoted to what is essentially the idea that a supervisor must ask a teacher to do their best day in and day out in a classroom, and be part of the continuous improvement process.

The continuing improvement process in New York State for schools in SURR status demanded that the district and a school based team identify the findings and articulate steps for implementing changes in that school. SED staff such as myself were then charged by the department to monitor the implementation on regular visits to the schools in accountability status. The district had to file multiple plans with SED to prove they were taking the accountability plan seriously —in the form of a CEP or Comprehensive Education Plan. Invented at SED by staff to ensure districts were identifying data, creating an action plan and monitoring improvement, the plan became one more document districts needed to fill out in the "Age of Accountability." From the creation of NCLB in 2001 to the present, schools and their staff spend chunks of time filling out plans, reports, and filing evaluations for everything from curriculum and instruction to money expenditures (Meier, 2004).

Out in the field as I was monitoring these SURR schools on the very intensive week-long visits, and I saw firsthand the pressure the administrators were under. They needed to do well with the district and SED. They wanted to hear that their initial fears were correct. They wanted to know their efforts weren't in vain. Their jobs and livelihoods were on the line. I saw how much stress they were under, as the tears flowed when we would have our initial meeting to convey the severity of the problems. Many knew how bad it was, but had no idea how to fix the problem by themselves, or by the teams handed to them by the districts we investigated.

There is a theory called transformational leadership that invests principals with almost super being levels of power to make changes. A transformational leader can motivate the unmotivated, encourage the despondent, and cure the sick. It's almost biblical (Bass, 1990). Like every good theory, this one has its flaws. A transformational leader cannot do it alone. There must be a team. I saw a number of very smart leaders, very dedicated leaders. I also saw poor leaders and checked out leaders. What I failed to see were people in the system who were willing to stand up to the status quo and make it stop. Educational systems, I have found, tend to thrive with the status quo, and changing systems is hard, long, difficult work (Wurdinger, 2018). In these SURR schools, the investment follows a Horace's compromise: do not ask for too much from us, and we will not ask too much from you. You could hear in the interviews and read in the document reviews the undertones of defiance in some of the schools (Sizer, 2004).

A theory I am fond of using to explain what people say away from authority is "hidden transcripts" (Scott, 1990). Behind every controlling regime's public story, there is a not so visible or auditorily counter script. On school improvement visits, the schools and the selected favored students and teachers tried to tell us of all the "good" in the school. Other teachers in random, hushed conversations would tell the state monitors about "the bad" which happened every day. The "hidden transcript" within these schools in trouble was the same: it's really the kid's fault. Not mine. It's someone else's fault : not mine. Critics would, could, or might blame tenure. Really it's not tenure. Nor is it the teachers unions. The flaw lies in the system that promotes the status quo. The system that sees the same demands placed on teachers from 1970 get bumped out of the way for demands well beyond their training.

A number of schools were determined to engage in trauma informed teaching and anti-bullying. Restorative justice has also made its way into our schools. What does this all mean? It is finally a realization that teachers were not trained as social workers and need help dealing with children who live in almost literal war zones or suffer from such immense poverty that they need help beyond what is currently in schools. It goes back to Maslow: If I feel safe, I can progress up the pyramid. If I am full, I can climb higher. Lyon (2020) has some great insight into the role of classroom engagement and supporting students. I also recommend teachers have McAllister (2020) children's book on how to say they are sorry. These two references are really powerful.

My second great take-away involved the really passive nature teaching and learning took in many classrooms. Not only did teachers in some instances not teach, but students sat there and took it. For many students, the idea was to allow time to pass, comply as minimally as possible, and escape back to the more entertaining hallways and cafeteria. There were few students engaged in group projects, even less engaged in active collaboration or discussion. The teachers in these classrooms were trying really hard to maintain some semblance of old-school order with quiet and compliance. This challenges all of the instructional learning which academics and practitioners call forth in the classroom. While builders, makerspaces, and innovation became fashionable a decade after I was in these buildings, there was no dearth of research at that time calling for teachers to create small group instructional opportunities. It is so very true that learning in these urban environments was more like practice for prison, and a number of research studies have discussed the school- to- prison pipeline (Morgan, 2021).

Engaging in this work at SED and being in the field allowed me to try and do what I could to help others at all times. But it was taking a toll professionally and personally. The constant driving around the state strained me to my limit. And I began to experience anxiety attacks on a regular basis. These schools were in such bad shape, and I took it personally. I felt a deep sense of responsibility for helping districts make changes and do a better job when they could to educate children. I learned by watching field based administrators and fellow staff that there was a huge communications gap between the central bureaucracy and the people on the ground. We had no implementation power in the department, and the schools were unable to implement. It was a classical example of a street level bureaucrat interfering with the best laid plans of policy makers (Jakubowski, 2020).

REFLECTIONS:

- How do you define a successful school?
- As a classroom teacher/administrator, how do you build bridges to improve communication at your school?

[12]

A SCHOLAR'S TURN

Have you ever thought, "I should go into administration?" Now is your time! Look at my journey to begin reflecting on what you could do. The demands are different, and the chapter tells you the story.

Guiding question: How do you dream of making change? To the system? To yourself?

As I embarked on this journey at three different education levels: K-12 school, college and then state level policy making, I wondered where it all went to or meant? As I finished my mentoring certificate in 2008, I embarked on a joint PhD- Advanced Certificate in Educational Leadership program at SUNY Albany. Almost 10 years later, I finished my Phd (Jakubowski, 2020), examining the role communication plays in rural school consolidation. I have also continued to write peer-reviewed articles for academic journals (Jakubowski, 2016; Jakubowski, 2017; Jakubowski, 2019; Jakubowski, 2019). I am, however, finding the peer-review process frustrating.

Often in the academic world, there is a call for theory. How does the paper relate to theory? How does the paper relate to data collection methods? There is often little thought put into the actual story. Maybe it's my training as a historian—or my storyteller's genes from my parents, but I want to have a great story. I need a story. Theory does not help me much. Nor does the method. I understand the significance behind collecting theory and methodology, but if the story is missing, then why bother?

The first three courses of my doctorate were all focused on work I was doing day- to-day: Ed Law, School Board and Community Relations, and the State and Federal Policy class. These three classes, right in the middle of the events I was working on while at State Ed, allowed me to see the theory behind practice of what was happening in reality with the books I read for class. For almost two years, I then worked on classes which were required as core. In these classes, I saw the ways in which organizations approached goal setting and problem solving. Practical books were part of my education as well. These works provided crucial understanding to the difficulties organizations face when they are trying to make changes. For all of the platitudes in the books, there is some truth to the idea of celebrating success and creating trust among a team. I saw that firsthand in the districts I served. There were limited times of trust among the team. For many, the role the administrators play is an ongoing jockeying for position, with each seeking favor with the Board of Education for career advancement.

These recurring dramas offered classical examples of court life from Europe. Instead of a Louis XIV, the administrators who approached as supplicants were using the personal connections that Bolman & Deal (2017) describe as part of the dysfunction of poor organizations. As board election results trickled into districts, jockeying for position resumed. In one district a whole team of senior leaders was let go, and a new team was brought in between May and July 1. This rapid and frequent example of instability among larger schools is addressed in research (Alsbury, 2008). The New York State Council for School Superintendents in their survey talks about board-superintendent relationship as one of the leading causes of churn. When administrators churn, the school goals, visions, and program plans are disrupted. A sports analogy: a football coach is fired after only two years, and a new group is brought in with a different philosophy. The organization quite often does not make the playoffs. Learning about the leadership theories and trying to understand the issues facing these schools during the first few years brought me to understand how impactful change at the top is to a district. It also helped me realize that educators often do not celebrate the small successes. Politically speaking, a small win may not seem like a lot in the grand scheme of a 13-year educational experience for a child, but they do matter. In academics, we often measure progress with grades. We try to celebrate grades, but students don't know what they really mean. How tangible is a 75 to a student? What does a "C" really mean? And if those classroom grades are not aligned with state expectations on standards and assessments, then a false positive may be created.

RESEARCHING PASSION, RESEARCHING PRACTICE

As I continued my studies, I felt the tug of rural schools called to me as a way to explore issues in accountability (my day job) , teacher mentoring (my reflections), rural education (my passion), and social studies (my addiction). Surrounded at work by major policy decisions, and watching the reform movement from the front line for over seven years, I experienced significant cognitive dissonance. This became even more so after I read research and texts which indicated the change process took a lot longer than what we were forcing on schools and districts.

Change research, as well as my own personal research, started in organizational work. My reading in my PhD program made me realize that change happens if there is a concrete understanding of a plan by people tasked to implement the task at hand. For a number of people at the local level, and even in SED, change happens when careful thought and deliberative input is discussed and considered. We were now moving into an age of consultants, and quick changes. Instead of analyzing the SWOT (strengths, weaknesses, opportunities, and threats), it seemed as if we were changing policy and process for the sake of change.

One author really drove this point home for me: John Kottor. In his *Our Iceberg Is Melting* book (Kottor & Rathgber, 2006), he points out people will not accept how bad or difficult a situation is until the world breaks apart under their feet. His research sets the stage for identifying how the change process can make a difference in people's lives. First, there must be a shared vision among all the people that the status quo isn't going to work. Second, people must have facts. Third, the group must agree on a course, and finally it needs implementation support. In situations where the idea of failure isn't tolerated, and job performance is a personal attack, work cannot be accomplished.

I also learned that organizations, such as schools, need to look like what people expect for legitimacy. In schools—this point is especially true. If a school does not look like what parents want from it, they will not fully support its mission. A really great study by Haller, Nusser and Monk (1999) showed how local people have very different ideas about what makes a quality school than does the state education department. The idea that school rituals—bussing, sports, classes, desks, teachers and a principal—are ingrained into American memory and folklore were astonishing to me. How could the idea of ritual and sameness overwhelm what people saw—like performance data? That is the point however, about any institution—if you have gone through the motions for long enough, then change creates a bigger issue than the status quo. Mike Kammen's book *Mystic Chords of Memory (2011)* really highlighted for me the need for stability in an historical sense, and in a way a community sense. This work was reaffirmed by scholarship emerging from the new AERA Rural SIG members (cited above). The research clearly indicated schools are critical to the rural communities and people they serve. The school is the center of the community, and supplies more than identity; it often supplies a reason for being (Jakubowski, 2020).

In the large and small urban communities of the state—such as Buffalo, Rochester, Elmira, Geneva, Syracuse, Utica, Binghamton, Schenectady, Albany, Troy, Middletown, and Newburgh—the schools are the only place where children can have some of their most basic needs fulfilled. The school is warm in the winter, has running water, bathrooms, and has food. For a number of parents who are struggling to get by, the institution of school is meeting their needs. We observed how crucial and profound schools really are to at-risk and middle-class families during the 2020-2021 global Covid-19 Pandemic.

The state, however, views schools as an operation which will enact standards and educate students, thereby fulfilling the mission of the State Education Department: *raising the knowledge, skills and abilities* of all its citizens. The state's goal for schools is clearly what theorists call Human Capital (Robeyns, 2006). The state needs and wants children who can help the workforce, be contributing members in society, and be agile for changes in the economy's structure. One way that New York has attempted to make this goal a reality is the neo-liberal standards and assessment reform efforts (Cervone, 2017). As I learned about the reformers in the federal and state level, conflict emerged: was I a supporter of students or teachers? Then I realized this was a false dichotomy. Like the union strike breakers of the 1800s and early 1900s, I was mentally pitting two groups against each other. In reality, the change I sought at work and school was essentially the idea of doing your level best at what you do. This idea found its roots in the ideas of sociology.

Jonathan Kozol (cited above) has a great series of books which tell a desperate and dark story about urban schools in the U.S. Some of his works cover the very districts which I worked in. To Kozol, the schools failed students at the structural level. These districts were establishing a power structure that replicated what the community and nation at large demanded: low skill and low wage workers. Discussing these issues in *Learning How To Labor* (Willis, 1977) and *Working Class Without Work* (Weis, 1990) both books provide immense background to understand how working culture is created in cities throughout the west. Both books tell stories of post industrial students learning in schools how to assume roles in a society to which they were born into. They are part of a group which is not told the "hidden curriculum" to assume middle-class status. They must play their roles in society—and it starts in school.

I began to realize how damning our education system was at the core. I also, for the first time, was exposed to the privilege that I never knew I had as a white, middle class, college educated person. It was within this sociological framework that I really began to understand how communities across the state, and the nation, were suffering from systems which cut opportunity down to a narrowly defined path. Take a step off, and you are back to square one. I realized I had dodged a major bulliet when I divorced. That could have really derailed me. Instead, the family structure I could depend upon and the efforts my parents made to help me on my feet were part of a *Home Advantage* which Lareau (2000) so precisely describes in her study of families.

My foray into sociology has since been interrupted by a hard passion for political sciences. Somewhere in my schooling, I began to see a political element in sociology. Maybe it was my almost Poli Sci minor at Fredonia which re-awoke, or a realization that somewhere along the path decisions needed to be made to set the stage for the community. I needed to understand why. Working in the education policy field pressed me to think about how a policy becomes a driver behind what happens in a community.

From my own family and personal perspective, Western New York suffered sociologically, economically, and politically. Policies designed to help New York City flourish destroyed the rust belt and the smaller communities in the state's interior. Elmira is a classic example of how policies really hurt small communities. As I was beginning my love of politics, I reflected on New York's Southern Tier region. The anchor city is famous for its prison for Confederate POWs during the Civil War. It is home to Mark Twain's study at Elmira College, and the birthplace of Syracuse University's Ernie Davis. The community is also located along the Sullivan Campaign from the Revolutionary War. Four very significant events to which the city has every right to advertise and seek people to visit and study.

In the Civil War period, a policy decision was made by the US federal government to stop exchanging POW's with the confederates. Prior to this decision, prisoners were often exchanged on the promise of good behavior and sent back home. The US government, and the Confederates, established notorious prison camps. In the south, Andersonville became the site of horrid treatment of northern soldiers. The north had its own version located in Elmira. So bad were the conditions, the camp received the nickname of "Hellmira" (Percoco, 2011).

Mark Twain is an Americana author who was famous for his works on the south, as well as his witty jabs at the foolishness of governments and businesses. His study and collected papers in the Elmira College Library are an amazing resource to students who seek to understand the significance of Twain to the American experience. As a writer, Twain captured the spirit of rural small towns and the south from an empathetic perspective.

Ernie Davis won the Heisman Trophy, the first African American to do so. His story of courage, grace, and inspiration has led to his hometown memorializing his feats from the football field. For a number of Elmira area students, sports has been the way out of poverty and into the collegiate world. The Civil Rights Movement and the role sports played in groundbreaking changes to the American Psyche are critical, as students know about Jackie Robinson and other athletes, but need to see and understand how critical New York's southern tier was to the change.

The Sullivan Campaign ranks as one of the brutal military events of the American Revolution. Following the Cherry Valley massacre, the Americans implemented a "scorched earth" policy against the Iroquois villages along the Susquehanna and Chemung River Valleys. An American Army moved across New York's southern tier and decimated villages and corn fields along the way. The army was charged with breaking the Iroquois alliance with Britain, and scattering their civilian population as far and as wide as possible. The Sullivan Campaign opened this region of the southern tier to settlement by land-hungry New Englanders.

Elmira's location provided easy accessibility to the west and the east. Watersheds, canals, and railroads gave Elmira an ideal location for the formation of a number of manufacturing plants. To its west, Corning, NY became home to the Corning Glass works, and the region became home to an airflight museum. With a wide range of agriculture, proximity to major markets, and a transportation network, the city thrived, until the 1970s, with collapse of manufacturing in the "rustbelt." This in turn has created a high poverty zone in the community. The school system has gone from multiple high schools to only one. It, like other areas of New York in the southern tier, has seen wealth outmigration and population decline.

I began to explore a myriad of issues related to school improvement policies during this time. How are teachers recruited and trained? Why are some districts so rapid in their turnover? How does leadership at the top affect leadership across the district? As I dove deeper into this research, I realized there was a significant issue in how problems are identified in schools. This was my introduction to the policy process:

1. Identify a problem
2. Set the agenda
3. Make a plan

4. Research potential solutions
5. Implement solutions and
6. Evaluate.

My research started to concentrate on problem identification. Problem identification emerges from what John Kingdon (1984) describes as Agenda Setting. In Kingdon's work, an agenda is created by a group of governing people when three events happen, and someone shepherds the events to reality. Kingdon identifies the three parts of the decision-making process for agenda setting as problem identification, policy alternatives, and political occurrences. Learning agenda setting has helped me understand the significance behind who brings these three parts, or streams together: a policy entrepreneur, or the person who makes the agenda setting come together and move into the actual implementation phase.

I clearly began to see in my work at State Ed and in the field that there were many different problem sets, and this created disagreement. Some of the New Yorkers felt the problem involved expensive schools. Other New Yorkers, especially upstate felt downstate and Long Island received too much attention. Many believed the system was broken, and only disbanding unions and creating charter schools would solve the problem. Then a number of people felt that poverty was the real issue. Solve poverty and you solve the educational crisis in New York State. With so many people so upset about so many things, it became clear that fixing schools is a "Wicked Problem."

To the policy folks, a Wicked Problem (Corbett & Tinkham, 2014) is one without a clear solution. Wicked problems can't be readily fixed, especially when the other two stages of agenda setting are considered. There are so many policy alternatives available to decision makers that any single one could be a good choice. Or a really bad choice. For the state, just trying to stay in compliance with the federal government was an overriding concern. For many of the local school districts, offering children a chance at an education the community would support was their issue. For many parents, lowering taxes and having greater programming at the school was their issue. Within these three competing issues, the state had decided that the schools' compliance was the most important issue. And as we have seen, compliance in a local, high poverty school meant massive amounts of detailed paperwork, the ability to trace aid dollars, and meeting the state standard for test performance.

The agenda set by the Board of Regents, the Commissioner of Education, and the state all became intertwined when in 2008 the economy crashed and burned. Federally, the housing bubble burst and so launched the "Great Recession." In New York State, we are so dependent on state and federal dollars, mass panic flowed throughout the system. As the American Recovery and Reinvestment Act or ARRA made its way through the state, I was part of a number of teams developing a way to spend the money as effectively as possible. An economic priming the pump attempt by the federal government required the state to give money to districts by poverty rates. ARRA was driven by the idea that public service jobs could be saved and infrastructure projects could create some jobs. Alas, this did not happen, as the US economy dove into a multiple year recession. At the state level, we asked schools to identify jobs saved or created by this funding. We allowed schools to invest in new programs designed to help student achievement increase. Oversight was limited, primarily due to the need to get funding out. At the same time, a new monitoring plan came into play: Differentiated Accountability.

SQR, ESCA & JIT (PRESTIPINO, 2020)

As the accountability system and federal policy continued to evolve, our policy makers began to look at ways to help schools in different levels of trouble. In response to a number of monitoring and guidance, as well as an understanding that it does a school no good to let the accountability ramp up without support, we were tasked as a department to come up with a way to help out schools. Our first task was to identify, based on federal accountability levels, how we would provide technical assistance to schools and districts. This resulted in an added alphabet soup of acronyms concerning how "we are here to help" as a department.

When a school entered accountability, and was identified as a "school in need of improvement" the team, of which I was part of, we concluded were going to implement a "school quality review" or SQR. The SQR would be given to schools as a way to examine what was happening and offer suggestions for improvement. The state also decided to differentiate the levels of the identification status. A school that missed annual yearly progress by one subgroup was called a SINI-basic school. These schools often had issues with a single subgroup, such as students with disabilities. The department, realizing that the number of schools falling into accountability would be unmanageable by a single, centralized staff, asked local school districts to run the reviews. The districts examined student accountability data, lesson plans, curriculum documents, and sampled classroom activities. The district, usually an Assistant Superintendent, would then write the SQR report using a state generated template, and send the report to the local BOCES. The BOCES District Superintendent then reviewed the report and sent it to SED, where a liaison would file the report away until the School in Need of Improvement grant arrived. The grant, which was a federally mandated amount of money (called a 1003a grant)given to districts in order to fund improvement activities. Often the grants were small in the overall grand scheme of things—$30,000, or $60,000. These grant monies could not be used to pay for someone's salaries or supplant local district efforts. Instead, the monies were supposed to be used to supplement local efforts. For most of the districts, this meant that they used the money for one-shot professional development, stipends for extra tutoring, or purchasing new technology. Our job was to make sure the grant and the improvement plans were aligned with the reports. It was often a back and forth between the department and the schools to ensure monies were spent correctly. Often, the monies were tied up, and not released to the districts in timely fashions, so the districts needed to reallocate funds in a grant amendment.

For schools newly identified who had missed on a lot of subgroups, they received a visit from the State Education Department. The team I was on, including myself, would travel around the state and visit these schools on a 2-3 day visit. There, we would team with the local district leader in charge of curriculum and instruction and review mounds of paperwork, visit classrooms, interview teachers, and interview focus groups of students. We met with the building principal and the data teams to understand the issues the schools were facing and what outsiders could do to recommend changes. The highest level of newly identified schools, a SINI Comprehensive, missed their targets in the all student group, meaning overall every group in the school was having difficulty with state tests. Those 3-4 day visits were intensive, unnerving, and exhausting. It felt like we were doing a SURR visit, only without the support of a BOCES District Superintendent, the team of experts, and others. These SQR visits revealed the ongoing daily struggle many teachers had, and many students felt.

Often the focused and comprehensive SQRs were reaffirming to administrators in the building that the daily struggle to motivate and implement change was huge. No other profession asks so much from educators and gives them so little time. One of the districts I worked with was high poverty (60%). It had recently seen an influx of non-English speaking refugees from Eastern Europe. The district, in a fading industrial community, saw almost 40% yearly student turn-over. The teachers had a very difficult time with the self-contained special education students. Many children were really in need of intensive help, and in many instances were not well supported as they engaged in classrooms. These special needs children were with a new teacher and 4 aids in a classroom of 15 kids. One child suffered fetal alcohol syndrome. Another child had been severely abused and suffered from traumatic brain injury. As I sat in this teacher's classroom, watching her try to teach basic math to make change from a purchase, I could see the agony in her eyes, the exhaustion in the teacher assistant's eyes, and the smouldering anger in the district representative on the visit. Why?

Federal regulations on testing became the leading issue causing anger to educators in the field. The accountability status ascribed to districts and schools was determined by student performance onELA and math testing grades 3-8 and the Regents exam in high school. The federal government demanded schools use data to diagnose problems in the students' performance and correct them. At the time, the data systems, especially in our schools of accountability, were stone-aged. It took half a year to get results back on the tests. Often the data was presented in such a way that item analysis by students was unavailable in a usable way. And the feds wanted every child tested.

Federal regulations required that all children, including children with special needs, take the same test, without their federally mandated accommodations, as their peers. These tests are three hours in length, often given in the worst weather time of the year, and are multiple choice and essay. As any adult knows, taking a final exam from high school or college, this is what we asked our students to do. Every year from 3-8th grade. Additionally, our students could feel the anxiety from their teachers. It often didn't help that the schools, especially low performing ones, would also make the testing events into something more. They became a focus of the school for a week. Posters went up about test-taking strategies. Teachers switched instruction to test prep. The principal would use announcements to motivate. And some of the schools held test rallies. These rallies in the gym or cafeteria were almost to the level of a high school pep rally. Teachers wore "You can do it" type T-shirts. During testing week, the school took on stillnesses of a college campus during finals week.

Anxiety broke out. Student mental health issues and professional stress seeped out in these schools. District officials were baffled that regular kids were subjected to this level of testing. They were furious at testing regs for students with disabilities.

In addition to no legally required accommodations on the tests, all students except for the 2% lowest, most disabled students in a district, were required to take the state tests. As part of the federal government's plan to ensure that districts were not "hiding" weak students by classifying them as disabled, the feds made sure that only the most disabled were taking tests. For a number of our urban districts, this low number could nowhere near accommodate survivors of poor pre- and post-natal care. Nor did it recognize the concentration of special needs students in these older cities. And the older cities suffer from severe environmental degradation issues. As America realized these past few years, from the destruction wrought in New Orleans by Hurricane Katrina to the Flint, Michigan lead poisoning, our kids are in trouble. A statistic scared me: 42 % live in poverty (Wimer & Smeeding, 2017).

It's not just the deep inner cities. It's in the rural areas, the suburbs, the small cities. Children live in places where the walls of their residents are so thin, the cold seeps in. They go to school in 100-year old buildings with coal/ oil burning boilers. There is lead in the water, and lead in paint at home, and maybe even the schools. Almost all of the children I saw are resilient. They have "grit" as Angela Duckworth (2016) writes. They wake up and go to a school that is like a prison. One district I worked with wanted to buy metal detectors with its school improvement grant. Why? Because the district had a number of gangs in the neighborhood. Remember, this was 2007, just over 10 years ago, under the Bush administration.

The children have resilience from the reform efforts foisted upon them. For schools identified as a third year in need of Improvement, or corrective action, the state created External School Curriculum Audits. This intervention required schools to hire an outside group, using their 1003a school improvement money, to come in and evaluate the written, taught, and tested curriculum. These groups, many created by former superintendents or by college faculty members, would gather a multitude of documents from schools and write a report recommending significant changes to the school's programming. Quite often the reports found that the curriculum, both written and taught, did not align with state standards or with assessment guidelines. These reports often noted lack of rigor in the classroom. In some instances, a middle school I worked with in a small district did not have students complete higher level math aligned to the standards until the end of the school year. Almost seven months were devoted to reviewing materials from two years earlier. These curriculum audits often, coupled with internal review documents from previous reform efforts, like a LAP or Local Assistance Plan, or Title I school improvement plan, indicated reformers were often poorly implemented and frequently abandoned. One reason for this event is linked to the high turnover rates many small or poor districts experience at the superintendency level. Remember, if change takes five years, and the average time in office for the top leadership position is three years, then there is a mismatch.

When schools entered their fifth year of accountability, or were declared in Restructuring, the Department would send a Joint Intervention Team (JIT) into the district. A JIT, similar to an SQR, was a joint effort between the state and a district. Quite often the JIT would include fellow SED staff from other departments. The JIT visit was a full week visit which required extensive involvement with the district. The districts were also asked to hire an Outside Educational Expert, or OEE, who would serve as the team lead. The OEEs were often retired superintendents. We at the department had to screen the OEE candidates. In a few districts, the OEEs were well known to the schools, because they often had served as a consultant in the district previously. A JIT also replaced the SURR visits, and eliminated the need for a BOCES District Superintendent. Sometimes the OEE would ask for experts in different areas to assist in the reviews. In one example, we had a team of seven go into a medium-sized high school in the upstate area. Because of the way the accountability system worked previously, a non-title I school was exempted from the interventions and attention that the state would offer from its technical assistance centers, its staff, and improvement oversight. The district had three schools in accountability, the high school, which was the subject of our visit, the middle school, which was in and out of accountability, and one elementary school, which was just entering accountability. The superintendent was thoughtful, dedicated, had an amazing Assistant Superintendent, and was ready to stop the status quo.

In the end, major changes happened due to this JIT. Multiple layers of administration changed at the building and central office. Teachers and guidance counselors received a rude awakening about how basic the instruction was. In one advanced placement class, the students were all white, and all were middle class. They were not expected to write on the analytical level that the AP class demanded. There was no discussion, only lecture and Powerpoint slide. The teacher thought that technology integration happened because of the Powerpoint slides. Guidance counselors were all put on a corrective action plan, as graduation rates were lagging for children in poverty and minority students. College and career discussions did not happen until 11th grade. Students were tracked based on subjective criteria like recommendations, and test analysis was non-existent. The hardest part of the whole visit was seeing the apathy in the students' eyes. They were complying with bad instruction to make it through the day. They behaved themselves admirably. When we interviewed students, they told us to look at the caring and dedicated teachers. In those classrooms, we found posters. We found evidence of engagement, we found students excited to learn, even if it was remedial work. In those classes, we found creative displays which defied the limited resources in the room. In other classrooms, we found blank walls. We found worksheets. We found passive annoyance at the students who just "didn't get it."

The school district, a small city in an economically depressed area, was not lacking for resources. The building had just been refurbished. The science labs and library were state of the art. Students had access to an amazing amount of resources. They were in small class sizes. There was a great music, art, and athletic program. The district had stuff. What it didn't have was a driving vision of improvement. When we interviewed leadership and teachers in the school, a theme emerged which boggled our mind. The interviewed staff reported the school was "a pressure cooker" and the halls were rowdy and out of control. Other staff complained about the "urban problems" spread from the large city which was near. To the entire team, which had experience in different settings, this image the staff painted was in complete dissonance. Having served in difficult schools around the state, what was happening in this school was nothing like what was going on elsewhere. One member of our team, an expert in urban education, shook his head and commented that the faculty and staff would have never made it in the environment he grew up in and practiced his craft in.

I also experienced the vicious level of politics on these JIT visits, as the harshest and most pointed recommendations offered by the Outside Educational Experts were softened or changed. Back in the office, away from the children, the schools, the taxpayers, and the desperation of schools in trouble for 40 or more years, we were verbally asked to "soften" language from "should" or "must" to "consider" or "could." Each JIT school would receive a final, formal recommendation. These recommendations included closing the school, making significant leadership and staff changes (replace the principal and 50% of the staff), or make major curricular and instructional changes. Our recommendations were almost always influenced by district needs. The superintendents in some schools would request that we give them the harshest report possible so that they could move reform. Quite often these harshest observations and recommendations would be softened, so as to not upset the "local control and culture" of the school district. In New York, schooling is controlled by local decision-makers. School leadership needed to balance the needs, wants, and desires of the local population with the demands for improvement at State Ed and the policy makers in Albany and Washington D.C. Rey (2014) wrote a profoundly observant article on this subject. The author talked about the tensions at the local level between what the superintendent felt was best for the school and what the local population believed. While this research is situated in rural areas, the same holds true for urban areas. I also found in my 2020 dissertation the same effect. Often the pressures from the federal and state levels were very different from the perceptions of local level leaders and community members.

These JITS, ESCAs, and SQRs really proved a very old adage which Haller, Nusser, and Monk (cited above) wrote about in the 1980s. How the state sees a school is often very different than how the local population sees a school. As the economy continues to struggle, and political leadership at the state level continuously face millions of dollars passing through on the way to local schools, I found in my research that state leadership wanted efficiency and effectiveness, especially due to the large amount of dollars passing to local schools (Jakubowski, 2020). The governors want schools to improve so that new businesses can be attracted to the state. And the state leaders want smarter people who have better jobs in the state to improve the social capital through their jurisdictions.

After the season of visits, I returned back to the department, and curiosity got the better of me. I started to hunt down old files and reports on the schools we were working with. A bureaucracy is a pack-rat. We hold onto everything. Notes, correspondents, plans, agendas and minutes of meetings. Now in the electronic age, some of those records are disappearing and we lose a significant tool in the reconstruction of policy, especially at my former level. We also lack hindsight and we don't use history very well.

As I dug my way back into the 1990s, and in some instances the 1980s, I found reports written about some of these very same schools. Some were glowing reports about significant progress made in implementing the new New York State Regents Compact for Learning. Other reports addressed compliance with new state and federal regulations concerning grants or funds. Further records revealed correspondence from small and large communities around the state. Many raised issues of injustice: a child suspended, a teacher forced to resign. Others asked the state to investigate books used in classroom instruction—*A Wrinkle in Time* or *To Kill a Mockingbird*. I came to a startling conclusion. Like a play on Broadway, or a Shakespearean comedy, or the Catholic Mass, it was the same script. The actors and their accents were different. The inflection and emphasis had changed, but it was still the same. There were applications for grant programs which disappeared. There were meeting agendas to discuss new regulations and compliances. There were echoes from the first round of NCLB testing, asking for a waiver, because the district was still training the teachers on the new formats and expectations. There were cries from parents who felt that the state needed to reverse a principal or superintendent decision. Citizens protested new state led requirements forced on local schools.

AFTERWORD

I learned I was a small cog in the machine. I was devastated. When I left Buffalo State College for the State Ed Department, *Wicked* (Schwartz, 2003) was all the rage and its song "Defying Gravity" was a smash hit anthem for those who wanted to improve the world. Some of my friends and associates could not believe I would be given a wonderful opportunity to help improve the lives of children and the school system. I remember listening to the CD and soundtrack and really finding a sense of purpose with those words:

> *Something has changed within me*
> *Something is not the same*
> *I'm through with playing by the rules*
> *Of someone else's game*
> *Too late for second-guessing*
> *Too late to go back to sleep*
> *It's time to trust my instincts*
> *Close my eyes and leap!*
> *I'm through accepting limits*
> *'cause someone says they're so*

Some things I cannot change
But till I try, I'll never know!
Too long I've been afraid of
Losing love I guess I've lost
Well, if that's love
It comes at much too high a cost!
I'd sooner buy
Defying gravity
Kiss me goodbye
I'm defying gravity
And you can't pull me down

Powerful words. Powerful imagery. Now—almost 10 years later—overdone. In the heat of the moment, I had come to believe that with my training, my experiences, my achievements, I was going to defy gravity. I was going to help change the system. What I realized though is the system is really entrenched. "It is what it is" and "we can focus on moving the needle" is not the grand plan or the inspiring vision. Those words are the reality of the fully functioning machine. Our education system is broken at a most fundamental level and needs to change. The passion and vision and dedication that inspires many young people into service is beaten out of their very soul by systems designed to carry the status quo.

In the 1980s cartoons, *Transformers*, the leader of the good guys, or autobots, was named Optimus Prime. Loosely translated from Latin, this character is the first best. This leadership style—supporting, thoughtful, caring, and noble—inspired me. Optimus sacrificed himself to ensure his followers and loved ones survived (Jakubowski, 2020). As an Eagle Scout, you are told in the charge set to

have opportunities to be of service to others, through your school,
your work, and through Scouting, because you know what you can
accomplish.Your position, as you well know, is one of honor and

responsibility. You are a marked man. As an Eagle Scout, you have assumed a solemn obligation to do your duty to God, to Country, to your fellow Scouts, and to mankind in general. This is a great undertaking. As you live up to your obligations, you bring honor to yourself and to your brother Scouts. If you fail, you bring down the good name of all true and worthy Scouts.

Your responsibility goes beyond your fellow Scouts—to your Country and your God. America has many good things to give you and your children after you; but these good things depend on the qualities she instills in her citizens. You are prepared to help America in all that she needs most. She has a great past, and you are here to make her future greater.

I charge you to undertake your citizenship with a solemn dedication. Be a leader, but lead only toward the best. Lift up every task you do and every office you hold to the high level of service to God and your fellow men -- to finest living. We have too many who use their strength and their intellect to exploit others for selfish gains. I charge you to be among those who dedicate their skills and ability to the common good.

It is profound to listen to as a 16-year-old to these words. It is a profound and solemn obligation to deliver these words to another young person. I also remember words from *The West Wing, a* television program which talked about leadership and the ability to make change. A quote by one of the characters drives the point home:

Toby Ziegler: One victory in a year stinks in the life of an administration. But it's not the ones we lose that bother me, Leo, it's the ones we don't suit up for." It's the ones we don't suit up for..." (West Wing, 2000 Season I, Episode 19).

In my almost 20 years I have suited up for battles. I suited up for those kids in my first job. I suited up for the kids in my second job. I went to battle in inner city schools as part of a grant program. When I went into state service, I thought this was my chance. We can really make a difference. When I entered graduate school, frustrated at the system, I found many of the same value system, who have told their stories before me. Sometimes better, cleaner, and clearer. Shirley Brice Heath, in *Ways with Words* (1983) opened my eyes to the language deficit poor children experience from the start. By the time they reach school, their vocabulary is already 100,000 words behind their peers. And it stems from how children and adults interact. Does the parent talk about them? To them? Or with them? In *Freakonomics* (Dunbar & Levitt, 2005) we learn that children in wealthier homes have more access to books, and grow up more interested in reading and farther ahead of their poorer peers.

The wealthy, the middle class, and the privileged have moved away from their neighbors, creating *Cities Without Suburbs* as David Rusk (1993) describes many of the rust belt cities, especially Syracuse, New York. As the wealthier families left the city, and the middle class moved away, the cities in the north died on the vine. One mayor pegged the infrastructure upgrades to her city at One Billion Dollars alone. That is just to make the roads and bridges and water and electricity safe. Other works call out the sociological destruction many poor and minority groups have experienced. Goyette's *Education in America* (2017) makes a great read for those who want to understand some of the leading problems facing students in schools.

In some of my research, and my experiences, going on field trips was once a key feature in education. From the Genesee Country Museum to the Buffalo Zoo, and Chicago and Detroit to see the treasures of a king from Egypt, it all helped. Now, we don't have field trips. In some schools, toilet paper and good food are luxuries.

I felt like I let down my Eagle Scout Charge. I feel as if I haven't lived up to my Vigil Honor promise. I had an opportunity to make a change and I feel like I couldn't because I was a cog in a machine.

But then a very good friend of mine reminded me of the critical nature of these cogs. Pointing out the purpose of a cog is to make change. In the machine, in the system. Status quo without a cog means work will not get done. Productivity will fall, and goals will not be met. A cog may not see what the grand plan or movement is at the moment, but later they will see it. I have had a few experiences when I realized that I did make a difference.

As I was in between jobs a few years ago, I was interviewing in a small rural district near the Pennsylvania border. I was in the running as a finalist for the Assistant Superintendent of Curriculum essentially. Leaving the first interview, I saw one of my former students waiting for a screening interview as well. This student had the baby in 10th grade. She was working two jobs to support herself. Yet here she was, a candidate for the second highest school administrative position in one of the largest regional school systems. She said "Hi" as I left. "I remember you—you were my Econ teacher in school." Almost 20 years later, she remembered me.

The second time was on the campus of SUNY Albany. As I was leaving class for my PhD studies, I heard my name "Dr. J! Dr.J!" Slightly confused, I didn't recognize the person until they reminded me who they were. Our conversation involved catching up, and he told me how interesting I made world politics for 10th grade. Now, he was studying for a Master's in International Relations because I got him interested.

The third time was back in Norwich, NY. I stopped in a store to grab a bite to eat. One of the counter people tilted her head and said, "Weren't you my history teacher?" Then it flooded back to me. One of my students in my Global 10 class my second year in the district. As we caught up, she told me how much she loved classes. The lessons were amazing and she loved how entertaining I was. The greatest compliment she paid me was her recollection. I was always concerned about the student's well being, one of the few teachers who cared about the charges in the classroom, in her opinion.

My time as a cog in the wheel has taught me the importance of finding what Simon Sinek (2009) calls your "why." As we roll out reform movements, and call for better leadership, efficient leadership, powerful leadership, it is critical to remember servant leadership. As Robert Greenleaf tells us in his book, *Servant Leadership* (1977), it is imperative to remember not only to be kind, but to care, and to do what needs doing. Thank you for listening to my story.

Now—Write your own story! Create your life map. Interact with the questions. Be a person who is a cog, a great magnificent, shiny world altering cog!

WHAT I WILL DO ON MONDAY:

WHAT I WILL DO NEXT WEEK:

WHAT I WILL DO NEXT MONTH:

WHAT I WILL DO NEXT YEAR:

I SEE MYSELF IN FIVE YEARS:

IN TEN YEARS, THESE CHANGES CAN BE TRACED TO ME:

WHEN I RETIRE, PEOPLE WILL SAY......

REFERENCES

Alsbury, T. L. (2008). School board member and superintendent turnover and the influence on student achievement: An application of the dissatisfaction theory. *Leadership and Policy in Schools, 7*(2), 202-229.

Bass, Bernard M. (1990). "From transactional to transformational leadership: Learning to share the vision". *Organizational Dynamics, 18*(3), 19–31.

Bolman, L. G., & Deal, T. E. (2017). *Reframing organizations*. San Francisco, CA: Jossey-Bass.

Carr, P. J., & Kefalas, M. J. (2009). *Hollowing out the middle: The rural brain drain and what it means for America*. Boston: Beacon Press.

Cervone, J. A. (2017). *Corporatizing rural education: Neoliberal globalization and reaction in the United States.* Springer.

Chamberlain, R. (2020). "Stronger With Each Other": A Case Study of a Shared Superintendency and Multi-District Partnership in Rural Minnesota. Unpublished PhD Diss. University of Minnesota.

Chokshi, S., & Fernandez, C. (2004). Challenges to importing Japanese lesson study: Concerns, misconceptions, and nuances. *Phi Delta Kappan, 85*(7), 520-525.

Corbett, M. (2007). Learning to leave: The irony of schooling in a coastal community. Halifax, NS: Fernwood Publishers.

Corbett, M., & Tinkham, J. (2014). Small schools in a big world: Thinking about a wicked problem. *Alberta Journal of Educational Research, 60*(4), 691-707.

Dias-Lacy, S. L., & Guirguis, R. V. (2017). Challenges for New Teachers and Ways of Coping with Them. *Journal of Education and Learning, 6*(3), 265-272.

Dunbar, S. & S. Levitt (2005). *Freakonomics.* New York: William Morrow.

Duckworth,A. (2016). *Grit.* NY:Scribner

Duncan, C. M. (1999). *Worlds apart: Why poverty persists in rural America.* New Haven, CT: Yale University Press.

Evans, R. (1996). The Human Side of School Change: Reform, Resistance, and the Real-Life Problems of Innovation. San Francisco, CA: Jossey-Bass Inc,

Folts, J. D. (1996). History of the University of the State of New York and the State Education Department 1784-1996. Albany, NY: State Education Department.

Froehlich, M. (2018) *The Fire Within: Lessons from defeat that have inspired a passion for learning.* Alexandra, VA: Edumatch Publishing.

Froehlich, M. (2020). *Reignite the Flames.* Alexandra, VA: Edumatch Publishing.

Goyette, K. (2017). *Education in America.* Oakland, PA: University of California Press.

Greenleaf, R. (1977). *Servant Leadership.* Mahwah, NJ: Paulist Press.

Hadeed, K. (2017). *Permission to Screw Up.* NY: Penguin.

Haller, E., J. Nusser, & D. Monk (1999). Assessing school district quality. pp. 263-286. in Chalker, ed. *Leadership for Rural Schools.* Lanham, MD: Scarecrow

Heath, S.B. (1983). *Ways with Words.* Cambridge: Cambridge University Press.

Heins, M. (2009). "A pall of orthodoxy": The Painful Persistence of Loyalty Oaths. *Dissent, 56*(3), 63-72.

Holme, J. J., Finnigan, K. S., & Diem, S. (2016). Challenging boundaries, changing fate? Metropolitan inequality and the legacy of Milliken. *Teachers College Record, 118*(3), 1-40.

Jakubowski, C. T., & Kulka, L. (2016). Overcoming State Support for School Consolidation: How Schools in the Empire State react. *Journal of Inquiry and Action in Education, 8*(1), 4.

Jakubowski, C., & Jakubowski, E. (2017). Using Forge of Empires as a Social Studies Teaching Tool. *Oregon Journal of Social Studies,* 42.

Jakubowski, C. (2019). Urban-Normative Reforms Missing the Mark. *Australian and International Journal of Rural Education, 29*(3), 92-104.

Jakubowski, C. T. (2019). Ourselves, Our Rivals. In *Interdisciplinary Unsettlings of Place and Space* (pp. 101-115). Springer, Singapore.

Jakubowski, C. (2020). *Hidden Resistance.* Unpublished PhD Diss, SUNY Albany

Jakubowski, C. (2020). *Thinking About Teaching.* Alexandra VA: Edumatch Publishing.

Johnson, J. W. (2019). *Lift every voice and sing.* Bloomsbury Publishing USA.

Kammen, M. (2011). *Mystic chords of memory: The transformation of tradition in American culture.* Vintage.

Kingdon, J. (1984). *Agendas, Alternatives, and Public Policy.* Mahwah, NJL Pearson.

Kotter, J. P., & Rathgeber, H. (2006). *Our iceberg is melting: Changing and succeeding under any conditions.* Boston: Macmillan.

Kozol, J. (2012). *Savage inequalities: Children in America's schools.* NY: Crown.

Lareau, A. (2000). *Home advantage: Social class and parental intervention in elementary education.* Mahwah, NJ: Rowman & Littlefield Publishers.

Lehr, C. A., Hansen, A., Sinclair, M. F., & Christenson, S. L. (2003). Moving beyond dropout towards school completion: An integrative review of data-based interventions. *School Psychology Review*, 32(3), 342-364.

Lyon, H . (2020). *Engagement is not a unicorn, it's a narwhal.* Alexandra, VA: Edumatch.

McAllister, M. (2020). *I'm Sorry Story.* Alexandra, VA: Edumatch Publishing.

Meier, D. (2004). *Many children left behind: How the No Child Left Behind Act is damaging our children and our schools.* Boston: Beacon Press.

Miller, J. (2021) "Let's not Do Anything Drastic: Processes of Reproducing Rural Marginalization in Education Policy Decision-making." Unpublished PhD Diss, University of Kentucky.

Miller, L. C. (2012). Situating the rural teacher labor market in the broader context: A descriptive analysis of the market dynamics in New York State. *Journal of Research in Rural Education (Online)*, 27(13), 1.

Miller, J. M., & Youngs, P. (2021). Person-organization fit and first-year teacher retention in the United States. *Teaching and Teacher Education*, 97, 103226.

Mireles-Rios, R., & Becchio, J. A. (2018). The evaluation process, administrator feedback, and teacher self-efficacy. *Journal of School Leadership*, 28(4), 462-487.

Morgan, H. (2021). Restorative Justice and the School-to-Prison Pipeline: A Review of Existing Literature. *Education Sciences*, 11(4), 159.

Parton, C. (2020). *"Country-fied city or city-fied country?": The impact of place on rural out-migrated literacy teachers' identities and practices.* Unpublished PhDl dissertation, The University of Texas at Austin.

Percoco, J. (2011). Encountering the Complicated Legacy of Andersonville. *Social Education*, 75(6), 326-328.

Prestipino, A. M. (2020). *Exploring the Role of Secondary Principal Leadership in Advancing the School Improvement Process* (Doctoral dissertation, Sage Graduate School).

Ragins, B. R., & Verbos, A. K. (2017). Positive relationships in action: Relational mentoring and mentoring schemas in the workplace. In *Exploring positive relationships at work* (pp. 91-116). Psychology Press.

Ravitch, D., & Stoehr, L. A. (2017). *The death and life of the great American school system: How testing and choice are undermining education.* New York: Routledge.

Rey, J. C. (2014). The Rural Superintendency and the Need for a Critical Leadership of Place. *Journal of School Leadership*, 24(3).

Robeyns, I. (2006). Three models of education: Rights, capabilities and human capital. *Theory and research in education*, 4(1), 69-84.

Rothstein, R. (2015). The racial achievement gap, segregated schools, and segregated neighborhoods: A constitutional insult. *Race and social problems*, 7(1), 21-30.

Rusk, D. (1993). *Cities without suburbs.* Wilson Center.

Sahlberg, P. (2007). Education policies for raising student learning: The Finnish approach. *Journal of education policy*, 22(2), 147-171.

Scott, J. C. (1990). *Domination and the Arts of Resistance*. New Haven CT: Yale university press.

Sinek. S. (2009). *Start With Why*. NY: Portfolio.

Sizer, T. R. (2004). *Horace's compromise: the dilemma of the American high school: with a new preface*. Boston: Houghton Mifflin Harcourt.

Sherman, J., & Sage, R. (2011). Sending off all your good treasures: Rural schools, brain-drain, and community survival in the wake of economic collapse. *Journal of Research in Rural Education (Online)*, 26(11), 1.

Thier, M., Longhurst, J. M., Grant, P. D., & Hocking, J. E. (2021). Research Deserts: A Systematic Mapping Review of US Rural Education Definitions and Geographies. *Journal of Research in Rural Education (Online)*, 37(2), 1-24.

Thomas, A. R. (2012). *In Gotham's shadow: globalization and community change in central New York*. Albany, NY: SUNY Press.

Weis, L. (1990). *Working Class without work*. NY: Routledge.

Willis, P. (1977) *Learning How to Labor*. New York: Columbia.

Wimer, C., & Smeeding, T. M. (2017). USA child poverty: the impact of the Great Recession. *Children of Austerity: Impact of the Great Recession on Child Poverty in Rich Countries, 297.*

Wurdinger, S. D. (2018). *Changing the Status Quo: Courage to Challenge the Education System.* Mahwah, NJ: Rowman & Littlefield.

EduMatch

PUBLISHING

Made in the USA
Middletown, DE
06 March 2023

26202032R00104